DURHAM

THE PHOTOGRAPHIC COLLECTION

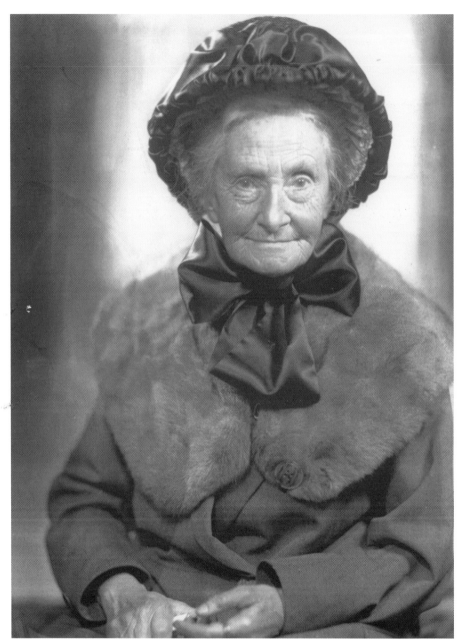

An exhibition photograph featuring an old lady, taken by Daisy Spence, *c.* 1928, the famous Durham photographer. She took over the business from her father John Reed Edis who first started in the 1890s in Gilesgate, moving to Saddler Street in 1899. Daisy's work was of a very high standard. She specialized in portraits and exhibited overseas as far away as the USA and Japan. Daisy is buried in St Giles' Churchyard.

DURHAM

THE PHOTOGRAPHIC COLLECTION

A COMPILATION OF
DURHAM PEOPLE & DURHAM AT WORK

BY MICHAEL RICHARDSON

SUTTON PUBLISHING

This edition first published in 2002 by
Sutton Publishing Limited · Phoenix Mill
Thrupp · Stroud · Gloucestershire · GL5 2BU

Durham People was first published in 1994 by Sutton Publishing Limited
Durham at Work was first published in 1995 by Sutton Publishing Limited

Copyright © Michael Richardson, 2002

All rights reserved. No part of this publication may be reproduced, stored in a retrieval system, or transmitted in any form or by any means, electronic, mechanical, photocopying, recording or otherwise, with the prior permission of the publisher and copyright holder.

British Library Cataloguing in Publication Data
A catalogue record for this book is available from the British Library.

ISBN 0 7509 3282 1

Typeset in 9/10pt Photina.
Typesetting and origination by
Sutton Publishing Limited.
Printed and bound in Great Britain by
J.H. Haynes & Co. Ltd, Sparkford.

Contents

Part One – Durham People

Part Two – Durham at Work

Part One
Durham People

George E. Summerscales, 1910. In the annals of Durham City Rugby Club the name of George Summerscales will be inscribed among the greatest. 'Summer' played his first game in 1896 at the age of seventeen. He made no fewer than fifty-one appearances in County Championship matches. Among his trophies was an international cap against the first All Blacks in 1905. The honour he prized most was when he skippered City to victory in the 1910 cup final against Hartlepool Rovers at Ashbrooke, their first success for twenty-two years.

Introduction

Durham is an enchanting city. In the words of Sir Nikolaus Pevsner, it is 'one of the great experiences of Europe. The group of cathedral, castle and monastery on the rock can only be compared to Avignon and Prague.' The peninsula with its high promontory is beautifully wooded and almost surrounded by the River Wear as it meanders to Sunderland and the North Sea; it is a memorable sight. Much of the charm of the city itself remains with its byways, despite the new road which tore the heart out of it in the 1960s.

Durham is of course an historic city. Where else is there a Romanesque cathedral built within the bailey of a Norman castle? In 1993, Durham Cathedral celebrated the 900th anniversary of its foundation, but a church had stood on the site since 995 when the monks had settled there to build a shrine for St Cuthbert, whose body they had brought from Lindisfarne more than a hundred years before to escape the Vikings. That settlement gave rise to a town, the millennium of which fell in 1995. Little wonder that the complex of the cathedral and the castle was declared a World Heritage site in 1987. The continuation of the spiritual and temporal side by side symbolizes the peculiar history of the area. In the Middle Ages the bishops had ruled the County Palatine like princes.

This collection of two hundred photographs and sketches, drawn from the archive developed by Michael Richardson in recent years, concentrates on the people rather than the place. The vast majority of the photographs have never been published before, and many local families are represented in the group and individual portraits.

Coal, mined in the region from Roman times, constituted the very life-blood of the county in the nineteenth and early twentieth centuries, and heavy industry dominated the region (but not the city) until Palmer's ironworks and shipyards closed in 1934, the prelude to the famous Jarrow March of 1936. The photograph of three young boys following their fathers into lives in the pits is for me especially poignant. The industrial production necessitated transport, by road, by sea, and by rail after the north-east pioneered railways in the 1820s. Great physical obstacles were overcome to provide the railway system by the Victorians, and the viaduct in Durham City, built on sand and completed in 1857, is an outstanding example of engineering skills as well as a beautiful object in its own right.

The Miners' Gala held on a Saturday in July, and now only tenuously surviving, was a great event in the city around the turn of the century. As a resident has recorded:

> We always went to see it, watching the proceedings from an upstairs window. During the morning contingents from the surrounding collieries streamed down the big bank from the station, each with its band playing and its huge banner carried by six men – two holding the poles and four the guy ropes. In the afternoon, the miners held their big meeting on the racecourse, and in the evening we watched them coming back up the North Road. But oh what a difference! The banners now lurched all over the road, and no doubt the music also reflected the men's state of mind and body.

Durham City, 20 miles from the coast but with good road and rail links, was a natural centre for military activities. The barracks, now the Vane-Tempest Hall, survive in Gilesgate as a reminder of past prowess, though many Durham men were too small for some regiments and had to join battalions based outside the county – the average height of

Durham recruits in 1914 was only 5 ft 4 in. The men of the area were particularly patriotic, though when the 8th Durham Light Infantry marched to the front in April 1915 few could have imagined that one-fifth of their number would be killed within a few days. They had responded to stirring calls from members of the local nobility and clergy.

Durham men and women, as Michael Richardson's photographs demonstrate, played as hard as they worked, gaining an enviable reputation for amateur dramatics and leek growing, celebrating national events and festivals with street parties, maypole dancing or morris dancing, and organizing annual events like the horse parade and the Miners' Gala which attracted attention from far outside the city.

The occupations of the residents of Durham City were on the one hand miners, craftsmen and manual workers, for the expansion of the iron and coal trade had brought a lot of artisans to the county, and on the other hand professionals, churchmen, academics and scholars of the cathedral and university. In between these two categories were the traders and shopkeepers of all kinds who served both. The university remained small until its separation from Newcastle in 1963, but there were the training colleges – Bede from 1838, St Hild's from 1858 and Neville's Cross from 1922 – and as the county town Durham was also an administrative centre. In 1939 the city had an insured population of 18,500; 12 per cent were in coal mining, 14.3 per cent in the distributive trades and 10.9 per cent in professional services. Consequently, Michael Richardson has photographs of people who followed a great range of occupations – chemists and roadworkers, hawkers and horse dealers, coal deputies and coach proprietors. Some of the occupations were rural, for Durham remains a small city and the countryside is not far away. For centuries the countryside extended on the south to the very foot of the cathedral. As in rural districts, most working-class families kept a pig to supplement their diet, and as late as the 1950s Durham was famous for its horse fairs.

Hilda Wilson Davison, who was a regular visitor to her grandparents in the city in the early 1900s, has written in a private memoir: 'I don't remember ever seeing a motor vehicle in those early days; all the traffic was horse-drawn. Private buses from the main hotels used to go up to the station to meet the trains; and the 'Black Maria' was a common sight, carrying prisoners from the station to the Gaol. It was a black van with a little barred window high up on one side, and at the back a policeman sat on a small seat outside the vehicle.' Michael Richardson has a photograph of the van in this collection.

The coming of the assize judge was another event in the city's calendar. He was conveyed in near regal splendour – an ornate closed carriage drawn by two horses, with wigged coachman on the box and two footmen standing behind. All three men were in elaborate uniforms, but the soberly dressed judge must have been a disappointment to onlookers! When the assizes were about to begin, two trumpeters would blow a fanfare outside the court. People believed that the fanfare was saying: 'He that is clear, Need not fear, For the judge is near.'

The city and its residents experienced poverty as well as prosperity. The worst year of the slump was in fact 1932 when two in every five of County Durham's insured population were unemployed. Indeed, unemployment in the north-east remained persistently higher than the national average, and local wages to this day are generally lower than in other parts of the kingdom. The bleakness of some of the urban scenes, as in a picture of Gilesgate Moor in the collection, symbolizes the low standard of living which prevailed even in fairly recent times. The slum clearance policy of the local council in the 1930s was too little too late, and there is independent testimony to the harshness of conditions in the city before and immediately after the Second World War.

Durham people are a resilient group, rightly proud of their traditions, and this book is a tribute to them and to the special ethos of the district.

Professor G.R. Batho

1
Meet the People

*Mrs Sally Savage from 27 Sherburn Road, early
1950s. This view is taken at the family allotment.
It was quite common in County Durham for
householders to supplement their diet by having a
domestic pig. Everything would be used apart from
its squeak.*

Just a Line to Say:

If you want a first-class Photo or Enlargement of yourself, or from a copy, you can obtain all you require at the Science & Art Photo Co., 69, Saddler Street, Durham. Outdoor Groups a Speciality, and having the largest Studio in the North of England groups can be taken inside in any weather. Prices are as low as possible for good work. You can get Photos from 3s. 6d. per dozen. Any Enquiry will have the personal attention of

Yours truly,

Geo. Fillingham,

Manager.

P.S.—Photos in this Guide taken by the Science & Art Co.

Photo by Science & Art Co.   *Durham.*

An advertisement for the Science and Art Company, 69 Saddler Street, *c.* 1909, the manager being George Fillingham. It was Durham's longest surviving photography business. It closed in March 2000 after almost ninety years.

John George Blackburn, cab proprietor, 50 Dragon Villa, Durham, 1890s. Mr Blackburn arranged pleasure parties, school trips, weddings and funerals. He was also a leading local preacher and took great interest in the local Primitive Methodist Church at Dragon Villa.

John Willy Pattinson, *c.* 1910. A prominent Salvation Army leader, he owned and ran the Dunelm Café in Old Elvet. In 1927 he was baking 28,000 loaves of bread per month. He was mayor of the city in 1930 and had the honorary freedom of the city conferred on him by the town council in 1950. In St Nicholas' Church a fine stained-glass window showing the Salvation Army crest was erected in 1963 in memory of Alderman Pattinson and his wife.

Golden Wedding photograph of Joseph and Alice Chapelow, May 1927. Joseph had a chemist's shop at 14 Claypath; he was also a photographer. He bottled and sold aerated waters at his shop and his bottles are now very rare. The Chapelows were strongly connected with St Giles' Church. Joseph, who was church warden, was also in the choir for many years. His wife was a long-standing member of the Mothers' Union.

William Henderson, FRHistS, *c.* 1874. William ran Henderson's Carpet Factory with his brother John. He was author of *The Folklore of the Northern Counties of England and the Borders*, 1866, and *Notes and Reminiscences of My Life as an Angler*, 1876. He was mayor of the city in 1849 and helped to raise money by public subscription for the building of the new town hall.

The Right Revd Handley Carr Glyn Moule, *c.* 1910, Bishop of Durham 1901–20. From 1898 he was honorary chaplain to Queen Victoria and on her death in 1901 was appointed chaplain-in-ordinary to Edward VII.

Edward Cummings, farrier, cartwright and general smith, 1920s. On the left is Edward Cummings and right is David Young, lamp oil man from the Coach Opening. The Coach Opening stood to the left of the Three Horse Shoes, Gilesgate. The name originated from the Railway Coach, an old public house which had stood on the site before the Three Horse Shoes.

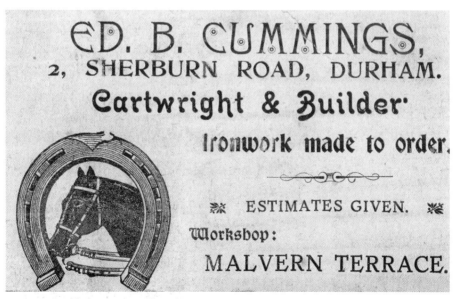

Business card belonging to Edward B. Cummings, 1920s.

Mrs Hopps polishing a copper jug in the Wheatsheaf public house, 3 Claypath, *c.* 1949. Mrs Hopps lived at Old Durham Farm. In the early 1960s Durham lost many old public houses because of the new road system.

Cycle dealer, Benny Clark, 85 Claypath, *c.* 1949. Benny also had a toy stall at Durham Indoor Market. At one time the property was a showroom for Lowes Marble Works and in 1936 an office for the British Union of Fascists (Mosley's Blackshirts). It is now a newsagent's.

The Savage family from Gilesgate in their Sunday best, 1903. Frederick Thomas (F.T.) Savage was originally from Hallgarth Street where he was a deputy at Elvet Colliery. He had a distinguished army record, having joined the Durham Rifle Volunteers as far back as 1873. He had more than forty years' service with the volunteers and later the Territorial Army. Left to right: Margaret Ethelina, Minnie, Frederick Thomas (father), Richard Ethelbert, Sarah Jane, John, Isabella (mother, née Button), James Edward (the author's grandfather), Alfred Septimus. This was a studio group taken by the Science and Art Company of 69 Saddler Street, Durham.

James Button (the author's great-great-grandfather) in his working clothes as a rail platelayer at Belmont, *c.* 1881. When James lived in Gilesgate in 1861 he was listed as a seaman; in 1871 he was a hawker of earthenware. He later moved to Belmont and lived at Old Station House.

Mary Button, née Burnside, wife of James Button, is seen here, *c.* 1896, with her granddaughter Mary. It is interesting to see the style of the costumes of that period.

Charles William Savage and family (son of F.T. Savage), 1917, 27 Alma Place, Gilesgate Moor. William enlisted in 1898 in the 1st Kings Dragoon Guards. He saw service in South Africa in the Boer War and later in the First World War. He was discharged in August 1915, on account of his wounds. His son William, standing to his right, was killed at Sherburn House Colliery in September 1923 aged sixteen.

Mrs Sarah Jane Savage, (daughter of F.T. Savage) general dealer, 24 Marshall Terrace, Gilesgate Moor, 1972. Mrs Savage started the business just after the Second World War. She ran one of the original open-all-hours shops. She sold almost everything from a pin to a bag of coal. Sarah married her cousin, William Savage.

Dean Alington and his wife in retirement in Hertfordshire, *c.* 1953. Dean Alington, dean of Durham 1933–51, was behind the setting up of Alington House Community Centre in the North Bailey and author of many books. In 1943 he founded the Durham City Trust. He had been headmaster of Eton before he became dean. His dog was named Mu after the Mothers' Union.

William Arthur Hall Shepherd, mayor of the city, 1957. He had also been mayor in 1943. He was born at Neville's Cross and was in business as a master tailor. His daughter was mayoress during both terms of office.

John William Blackburn, cab proprietor, 50 Dragon Villa, Sherburn Road, *c.* 1949. John Willy took over his father's business and with his bus, the *Dragon Queen*, he served the local villages. He was also on the Belmont Parish Council for many years.

Mr George Rolling, fruit and vegetable dealer, 1920s. He later opened a shop on Sunderland Road near Edge Court, Gilesgate. Later still, when business was flourishing, he had a shop built at 45a Sunderland Road, now Alan's Hairdressers. The small hatch at the bottom left-hand corner was where the ash toilets were emptied.

Mr Smith outside his butcher's shop at 88A Claypath, 1899. Open windows were common for butchers and fishmongers in the city until the late 1940s.

Nichol Chilton outside his shop, 26 Sherburn Road, Gilesgate, *c.* 1914. Nichol was born in Gilesgate. His son Thomas took over the business which lasted until the early 1970s. Donald Crampton, who had a successful business in New Elvet, was a grandson and Ruth Heslop, who had a shop near the Green in Gilesgate, was Nichol's daughter.

The Pattison family in the garden of Ivy Cottage, which stood in the grounds of the Girls' High School near Brown's Boat House, *c.* 1913. It is interesting to see children's toys of the period. Back row, left to right: Joseph William Pattison, Janet Pattison. Middle row: Mary Isobella Pattison, Marjory Hornsby, Margaret Emily Pattison. Front row: Thomas William Pattison and Dorothy Hornsby (the Hornsbys lived at the Drill Hall, Gilesgate).

The Revd H.E. Fox MA, vicar of St Nicholas' Church from 1882 to 1895. Fox succeeded his uncle the Revd George Townsend Fox, vicar from 1856 to 1882. It was his uncle who paid for the erection of the spire at his own expense.

L/Cpl. Richard Savage, 10th Royal Hussars, c. 1917. Richard is seen here with his wife, Annie, who was a maid in Lord Kitchener's household. Richard met Annie while on leave in the south of England. Richard was born in Hallgarth Street, and later moved to Gilesgate as a child. In 1927, when Richard left the army, he was found a position in the Law Courts in London by an officer whose life he had saved in the First World War.

2

The Happiest Days
of their Lives

*Albert Richardson (great grandfather of the
author), head gardener at St Hild's College,
c. 1918. Until the 1950s gardening was taught
as part of the curriculum. At the college garden
show in 1922 Albert exhibited eighteen varieties
of potato grown in the college grounds.*

St Oswald's Infants' School, Church Street, *c.* 1895. To the right of the teacher is Alfred Septimus Savage.

St Hild's Model School, Gilesgate, *c.* 1897, opened 30 May 1864. This is one of only three known photographs taken by Joseph Chapelow, chemist, photographer and aerated water manufacturer of 14 Claypath.

A class from St Giles' Church of England School, *c.* 1901. The Revd Francis Thomas, vicar of St Giles, is standing on the far right. Back row, right, Alfred Septimus Savage and third row, right, Richard Ethelbert Savage. The school was known locally as the Gate School. St Giles' Filling Station now occupies the site.

Blue Coat girls, *c.* 1900. The teacher on the left is Miss Morgan and on the right is Mrs Fish, the headmistress. Back row, far right, is Nora Young.

A Midsummer Night's Dream performed by Durham Girls' Grammar School, Providence Row, *c.* 1927. The school is now Durham Sixth Form Centre.

Neville's Cross College, staff and seniors, *c.* 1929. The college was opened in September 1921. In 1939 it moved to Bede and later to Hatfield for the duration of the war, as the college was taken over by the War Office as a casualty clearing station.

A classroom scene at Blue Coat School, Claypath, around 1914. Front row, fourth from left, is Thomas William Pattison from Ivy Cottage.

Millburngate Nursery, 1951. It was built during the last war. The Millburngate shopping complex now occupies the site.

The staff from Whinney Hill School, *c.* 1957. Front row, centre, is Miss Viola Flemming, the headmistress. The school was officially opened by Brig. Gen. Sir Conyers Surtees on 15 September 1932.

Gilesgate Moor Junior Mixed School, Class 1, 1951. The school was also known locally as the 'Tin School' because it was constructed with corrugated iron sheets.

3
High Days and Holidays

*Blue Coat School, Claypath. Morris dancers at the
May Day festivals held in the schoolyard, 1963.
The first May Day festival was held in 1933.*

Frederick Menspeth Young, *c.* 1910, coachman to the high sheriffs of the county of Durham from 1897 until 1914. Mr Young was a cab driver at Peele's livery stables which stood behind the Royal County Hotel.

Whinney Hill with its glorious welcome to George V and Queen Mary, 10 October 1928.

Easter Fair on the Sands, Durham City, *c.* 1927. The Sands belong to the freemen of the city, and have been the site of fairs of all descriptions for hundreds of years.

Student Rag Week, Palace Green, 1948. Wood & Watson Ltd for many years loaned to the university students wagons and drivers for the carnival parades. The parades faded out in the early 1970s.

The grandstand which stood on The Racecourse, seen here on Regatta Day, *c*. 1885. The races dated back as far as 1665 and continued until 1887. In the distance is Whinney Hill.

Durham City Horse Parade travelling down Gilesgate Bank, *c.* 1910. The parade started at the barracks (Vane-Tempest Hall) and travelled through the city and then back to the barracks to be judged. This was an annual occasion, which involved many people and businesses in the city and the surrounding villages. The streets were lined with spectators for the show and the horse parade was an event comparable with the Miners' Gala.

Robert Ebdon, landlord of the Brewers Arms, 80 Gilesgate, and, on the right, Thomas Lee, *c.* 1913. They were entrants in the Durham City Horse Parade at the barracks.

George Rolling from the Co-operative Store in Claypath, *c.* 1909. He was an entrant in the horse parade. On his cart is a typical Edwardian bedroom suite complete with washstand.

Mrs Emily Studholme, manageress of the Rex Cinema, Gilesgate Moor. This photograph was taken on her last opening night at the Rex, 24 January 1958. The last film shown was the action-packed *Eagle Squadron*.

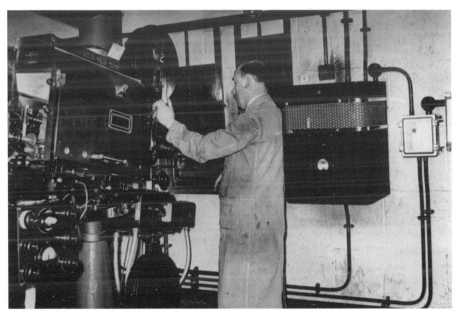

Mr Edgar Denham, projectionist at the Majestic Cinema on Sherburn Road Estate, *c.* 1952. The Majestic is now a bingo hall.

Visit of Her Royal Highness the Princess Elizabeth, 23 October 1947. The princess is seen here leaving the cathedral on Palace Green. Passes were issued by the town clerk, George Bull, and instructed the holder to hand them to the policeman on duty.

Durham Miners' Gala on the racecourse, c. 1949. The gala was at its peak in the late 1940s.

Miners' Gala, 1954, at Old Elvet. Visiting speakers that year were the Rt. Hon. Sir Hartley Shawcross QC, MP, the Rt. Hon. Nye Bevan MP and Bessie Braddock MP. The first Miners' Gala was held at Wharton Park, 12 August 1871. Each July thousands of coalminers and their families would take over the city for the day. The building on the left was the Dunelm Café, now part of the Royal County Hotel. The arched entrance on the left is that of Chapel Passage; this led to the old Methodist Chapel, built in 1808 and demolished in the 1960s.

An aerial view of Old Durham Gardens, *c.* 1949. In the 1920s Old Durham Gardens were a popular weekend attraction. They advertised dancing, a putting-green, a running track, tennis-courts and a tea garden. The Pineapple Inn was attached to the gardens. By 1926 it had lost its licence and thereafter only sold soft drinks. The original Hanging Gardens of Old Durham belonged to the manor house, which was inherited in 1630 by the Heaths of Kepier; the gazebo and walled garden are all that is left of the ancient house. In 1939 Mr Jack Hay from Gilesgate discovered fragments of Roman tiles in the nearby sand quarry. This led to the discovery of a Roman bath house. An archaeological dig was carried out, but sadly the remains were later destroyed by quarrying.

Empire Day at Blue Coat School, *c.* 1949. The first Empire Day was held in 1902. George Savage is in the front row, third from the left, dressed as John Bull.

Dancing around the Maypole on May Day in Blue Coat schoolyard, Claypath, *c.* 1963.

Children from Annand Road, Gilesgate, collecting a penny for the Guy, *c*. 1955. Left to right: Alan Greaves, Peter Hughes, Eddie Jenkins, Victor Richardson, Alan Dickson and Tony Greaves.

Victory in Europe Day, John Street, May 1945. John Street is near the city viaduct, and the railway embankment can be seen at the rear. The lack of men is quite noticeable. It was some time after VE Day before the soldiers were demobbed.

Victory in Europe Party held in Magdalene Street, Gilesgate, May 1945. The relief at the end of hostilities in Europe is evident on the faces of the people, though probably many had lost relatives and friends in the war. The boy third from the right in the front row is Frank Richardson, the author's father.

Sledging on the Observatory Field, *c.* 1947. Observatory Field has been a popular sledging spot since Victorian times. The field is now owned by Durham School.

The bandstand at Old Durham Gardens, *c.* 1933. This view was taken from the rear of what was the Pineapple Inn, now a private residence.

4
Leisure Pursuits

The Wheatsheaf Leek Club, 1957. The Wheatsheaf stood at the bottom of Claypath and was demolished to make way for the new through road.

The King William IV, which stood at the bottom of North Road, *c.* 1966. The solid oak front door was salvaged by Mrs Watson of Kepier Farm and is now the main door of the farmhouse.

The Five Ways Inn and Stanton's Fish and Chip Shop, 130 Millburngate, *c.* 1966. To the left can be seen the construction of Millburngate Bridge.

The Waterloo Hotel, 61 Old Elvet, *c.* 1964. It was here, in July 1820, that the body of John Lyon, Earl of Strathmore, lay in state while on its way to Gibside. The Royal County Hotel stands to the right. On the left is the old County Court built in 1871. In 1976 the new Elvet Bridge was erected.

The old Three Horse Shoes, 64 Framwellgate. This building was demolished in the early 1960s. On the right of the picture is the original site of the well, known as the Framwell head, which carried water to the pant in Durham Market Place.

Miss Ann and Miss Sarah Palmer (sisters), who ran Palmers Temperance Hotel, 4 North Road, *c.* 1926.

Palmers Temperance Hotel and Café, 4 North Road, *c.* 1900. On the right was the Primitive Methodist Chapel; the left side of the building is now Robinson's Pet Store.

The Durham Ox, 39 Gilesgate, *c.* 1933. This public house stood to the left of the Drill Hall at the bottom of Gilesgate Bank. At one time it was known as the Bull and Dog Inn. The public house got its name from the famous Durham Ox which was exhibited throughout England and Scotland in the late eighteenth century.

The 'Volunteer Arms' Hotel, 47 Gilesgate, *c.* 1935. The landlord was Vincent Tindale, seen here wearing a waistcoat. The hotel stood at the bottom of Gilesgate Bank, above Station Lane.

St Nicholas' Boys' Club, Claypath, seen here on a fishing trip, *c.* 1955.

St Nicholas' Church Choir outing. The picture was taken at Blackhall Rocks near Hartlepool on 17 July 1884 by the Revd H.E. Fox, vicar of the church and first chairman of the Durham City Camera Club, which was founded in 1892.

Gilesgate Scouts, *c.* 1947, at Vane-Tempest Hall on 'bob a job' week. The Gilesgate Scouts came into existence in about 1926.

The Gilesgate Archery Club, Gilesgate Welfare Association (Vane-Tempest Hall), *c.* 1947. Left to right: Cyril Walker, Dorothy Cole, Colin McGowan, J.E. Studholme, George Cole, ? Tiplady.

St Nicholas' Church Boys' Brigade, *c.* 1904, seen here in Blue Coat schoolyard, Claypath. The vicar is Mr Bottomley, the man with the beard. It is interesting to note that the boys are carrying rifles. Many lads from the Boys' Brigade were later killed during the First World War. In St Nicholas' Church the First World War memorial records the names of the brigade members who gave up their lives for king and country.

Mrs Alington and the Cathedral Widows in Alington House, *c.* 1951. The Cathedral Widows' origin goes back hundreds of years. Mrs Alington is seen holding flowers.

The Rover steam engine, *c.* 1962, built in 1913 and renovated by Mr George Flynn at his garage at the top of North Road.

National Telephone No. 69.
Telegrams : "COLPITTS, DURHAM."

"The ...
Criterion"

(Established 1848).

**Also at COLPITTS' and
STATION HOTELS. · · ·**

N.B.—Sole Proprietors of "CRI'
BLEND SCOTCH WHISKY,
3/6 per bottle.
41/- per dozen.

N.B.—COLPITTS' ALE
in pint screw stoppered
bottles, **2/9** per dozen.

T. & H. C. Colpitts,
Framwellgate Bridge,
... DURHAM.

The Criterion, Framwellgate Bridge, c. 1909. The Criterion, or the 'Cri' as it was known, was first established in 1848 by Mr Herbert Robson. In 1894 it was bought by Mr Thomas Colpitts and his cousin Mr T. Burton. The 'Cri' was described as a friendly place where a working man could relax in good company after a hard day's work.

St Nicholas' Church Boys' Club on one of their weekend trips, seen here near Kepier, c. 1955.

5
Sporting Life

Bede Model School rugby team, Gilesgate 1922. The New Bede Model School was built on Bede Bank at the west end of the college site and was opened on 20 February 1886. The Model School closed its doors for the last time in July 1933. The building was renamed Carter House after Miss Phyllis Carter and her father in 1985.

Gilesgate Moor Council School football team, 1921. The young lad in front of the teacher on the right is John Oliver from Gilesgate Moor. The school opened in 1905 and was later renamed Gilesgate Moor Junior Mixed.

Gilesgate Moor Council School football team, 1951. The deputy headmaster was Mr Kirk. Top row, left to right: J. Garfoot, B. Newby, B. Lumley, K. Bryan, B. Mansfield, B. Proctor, -?-. Bottom row: F. Richardson, B. Alderson, J. Bell, J. Lee, D. Ferguson, A. Gravestock.

St Oswald's football team, 1914. Many parishes in the city had their own football teams.

Mackay's Carpet Factory football team, *c.* 1949. Back row, left to right: John Mackay, Walter Shea, Tommy Little, Ken Johnson, Wilf Anderson, Tucker Metcalf, Tommy Sharpe, Wilf Helm, Percy Helm. Front row: Harold Buckston, Alan Davies, Gary Marley, Jim Crampton, John Cooper and the mascot, Wilf Anderson's son.

St Leonard's RC School football team, League Cup winners, 1953. The photograph was taken in the school grounds. Top row, left to right: M. O'Brian, M. Doran, R. Crawford, T. Hopper, F. Richardson, C. Davies, T. Kegan. Bottom row: E. Hutchinson, B. Barr, B. Bowes, J. Barret, D. Laing, B. Clark, A. Sutherland. The team strip was green and white.

Mackay's Carpet Factory football team, *c.* 1926. Top row, left to right: -?-, Jackie Walker, Bobby Allenby, Jackie Burnip, Bobby Allison. Middle row: Billy Renwick, John Killian, Bob MacMorran, Jimmy Crampton, Harry Aves. Front row: Jack Smith, Thomas Rowntree, -?-.

Bede College Swimming Club, 1933. Back row, left to right: H.H. Christian, J.E. Brigham, W.E. West, J.W. Martin, A. Wilson. Front row: J.C. Willcox, L.J. Webster, W. Nash, G.S. Webb, L.F. Mills.

Durham Wasps, 1950. The Wasps' origin goes back to 1942 when Canadian airmen were drafted into the area. In the early 1940s Durham had thirty-five Canadian National Hockey League Stars participating, with an average gate of ten spectators.

Johnston Technical School football team, April 1911. Photographed in the old Johnston schoolyard which stood at the bottom of South Street. Back row, left to right: A.R. Ramshaw, D.I. Raffles, W. Robinson, E. Alexander, A.W. Atkinson, S. Whalley, P.C. Brown, T. Barr, F.G. Cousins, G. Robinson, P.G. Frogley, W.J. Gibbons. Middle row: J. Hudson, H. Bennett, R.H. Ward, G. Ferguson, G. Hauxwell, J. Duke, J. Moreland. Front row: J.H. Hall, W. Davison, A. Addison.

Durham City Rugby Football Club, 1910, winners of the Senior County Cup. Top row, left to right: D. Crampton (Assistant Groundsman), E. Laws (Committee), Col. Turnbull (President), J. Boyd (Hon. Sec. and Treasurer), H.E. Ferens (County Rep.), J. Clark (Groundsman). Middle row: F. Marshall, C. Cranmer, W. Coulson, R. Salvin, J. Turnbull, W. Weavers, W. Cook, R. Bell, D. Elwood, M. Carlin, G. Miller, J. Phillips. Front row: J. Malpass, W. Weighman, H. Imrie, G. Summerscales (Capt.), H. Phillips (Vice-Capt), R. Long, T. Patterson, T. Walker.

Gilesgate Rugby Football Club, 1906. Top row, left to right: H. Thompson, P.C. Haggie, J. Forrester, A. Reed, B. Milbourne, J. Christie, T. Markham, W. Blagdon, L. Patterson, J.B. Tomlinson, H. Wise, E. Green, H. Smith. Middle row: T. Smith, G. Reed, T. Patterson, H. Alison, W.H. Wood, R.E. Coyne, M. Carling, A. Evison, K. Johnson. Front row: J. Allison, E. Whale, H. Cole, J. Harker, T. Lightfoot, G. Elliot, G. Rowell.

Henderson's Wanderers, Association Football Club, 1902. Henderson's had the carpet factory in the city before Mackay's. Back row, left to right: J. Hortin (Sec.), C. Hortin, W.E. Pounder, H.R. Turnbull, W. Crow, T. Baines (Trainer). Middle row: T. Rowntree, H. Dixon, S. Tulip, C. Matthews, A. Cleminson (Linesman). Front row: R.N. Gibson (Vice-Capt.), R. Williamson (Capt.), R. Bell.

6
Working Life

*Lockey's Supply Stores and Café,
76 Saddler Street, c. 1909. The Lockey family
were from Rossleigh House, Bede Bank, now the
principal's house for the College of St Hild and
St Bede. Frank jr, the son of the proprietor, was
killed on the Somme in 1916. The family grave
is in St Giles' 1870 Cemetery.*

A £5 bank note from Jonathan Backhouse & Co., Durham Bank, 1882. Durham Cathedral and Prebends Bridge are illustrated. These notes were hand signed; in this example the signature has been cut out. Jonathan Backhouse & Co. later amalgamated with Barclays Bank.

Plastering gang from Framwellgate, c. 1894. Top row, left to right: J. Palmer, J. Plimmer, T. Killian, W. Scott, H. Evans. Front row: A. Pearson, R.A. Pearson, Dick ?, T. Raybole, W. Baker.

George Pescod, dealer in horses, North Road, Durham, *c.* 1900. Durham was once famous for its horse fairs. The fairs faded out in the early 1950s.

Hayton's Novelty Bazaar, Durham Indoor Market, *c.* 1909. Hayton's stall was situated at the left-hand side of the market. The young girls are wearing the fashion of the day with skirts five inches above the ankle. The postcard photograph was sent to Eleanor from Polly, 22 Gilesgate, cancelling a trip to the Palace Theatre.

The staff from City of Durham Gas Company, Sidegate, c. 1910. The device in the centre of the photograph is for removing water from household gas pipes. Water would build up in the pipes and the lights would flicker and go dim.

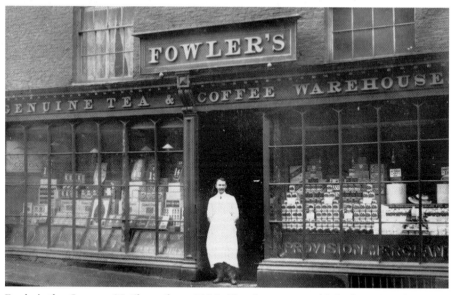

Fowler's the Grocers, 99 Claypath, c. 1914. The shop was established in 1841 by James Fowler, and his son Matthew is seen standing at the entrance. It was in the great miners' strike of 1844 that James Fowler came to the rescue of the Durham miners. He supported them to the best of his ability, and after the strike the miners in return gave him and his business great support. He soon became a man of influence, and was mayor of the city in 1872, 1881–3, 1886 and 1890.

JOHN LOWES & SONS, Monumental Masons and Sculptors,

Photo by Science & Art Co. *Durham.*

Have an exceptionally large stock of ARTIFICIAL WREATHS.

NAT. TEL. 128.

Showrooms—85, CLAYPATH
Works—180, GILESGATE

DURHAM.

Lowes' Marble Works, *c.* 1908, which stood at the bottom of Gilesgate Bank. In July 1904 Councillor Charles Lowes was killed by one of his apprentices in the building at the rear. He was buried in St Giles' 1870 Cemetery and his grave is marked by a fine, black granite headstone. The apprentice, Robert John Allen, was sentenced to twenty years' imprisonment in Durham Goal. Allen's father was in fact a prison warder at Durham. His girlfriend stood by him and after his release they emigrated to Australia.

Porter's Supply Stores, 43 Gilesgate, which stood to the right of the Drill Hall at the bottom of Gilesgate Bank, *c.* 1947. The manager, Mr Hale, is standing in the doorway. To the right is Station Lane and the back entrance to the 'Volunteer Arms' Hotel. The property was demolished in the 1960s for the new road.

Porter's van at the rear of Porter's, *c.* 1947. Robert Inglis is on the left and on the right is Fred Mulgrew.

Pattison's staff, *c.* 1905. The workforce is seen here outside the workshop behind the Royal County Hotel, Elvet Waterside. The furniture and upholstery business was founded in about 1874 by Mary Pattison. Mary's nephew Arthur Pattison, the large gentleman in the centre of the picture, took over the business. The establishment still operates from their retail shop, 16 Elvet Bridge.

Staff from the Durham City Laundry, which was situated near the Sands, *c.* 1925.

The Old Tea Pot was originally outside C.F. White's Wholesale Retailers in the Market Place around 1860. Later the family moved it to Gilesgate post office which stood about 20 yd down from the Old Drill Hall. The photograph shows Miss H. White and her sister Emma Vasey outside Gilesgate post office, *c.* 1899. The tea pot was moved to Fowler's the Grocers, Claypath, then later to the House of Andrews Bookshop, 73 Saddler Street.

H. J. Leeming, M.P.S., CASH CHEMIST and PHARMACIST . . . . .

Dispensing Department.

All Physicians' Prescriptions are Dispensed at Store Prices with the Purest and Freshest :: Drugs : : : : : Obtainable. : :

All Veterinary Medicines kept in Stock & Prepared according to Private Recipes.

Patent Medicines

at Store Prices

—:o:—

Toilet Articles
Tooth Brushes
Hair Brushes
Nail Brushes,
Tooth Powders
Perfumes, etc

Everything Stocked which belongs to a Modern Pharmacy

Photo by Science & Art Co.   *Durham*

Leeming's Ivy Leaf Corn Cure, Speedily and Painlessly removes obstinate Corns with two or three applications.

PRICE, 7½D.

STATION CUTTING, NORTH ROAD, DURHAM.

An advertisement for Leeming's Cash Chemist, *c.* 1909, which stood at 57 North Road. The property was demolished in the 1960s to make way for the new road system.

Rolling's the general dealers, 45a Sunderland Road, Gilesgate, *c.* 1949. The building is now Alan's Hairdressers.

Mountjoy Hill, showing Elvet Colliery to the left, *c.* 1897 (sunk in 1828). St Oswald's Church can be seen to the right. The church had to be restored in 1834 as a result of mining subsidence from Elvet Colliery. The colliery's main outlet was to local residents. It closed in 1908, mainly because of subterranean flooding and the cost of payments for property which had been damaged by subsidence. Durham University Main Library now occupies the site, opposite the New Inn on the Stockton Road.

Coulson's Boring Contractors, Margery Lane, Crossgate, *c.* 1920. Coulson's was a long established firm in the city and was involved in the opening of the Grange Iron Works at Carrville in 1866. The business in Crossgate continued under Coulson's name for many years.

Gilesgate's first ice-cream shop, 82 Gilesgate, *c.* 1912, which stood next door to the Brewers' Arms. The shop was owned by the Dimambro family who later moved to 90 Claypath. Charlie Dimambro is standing in front of the window.

Staff of Durham County Hospital at the Princess Ballroom in the Three Tuns Hotel. The dinner was held to mark the introduction of the National Health Service Act, 5 July 1948.

The unveiling of the Miners' Memorial at Durham Cathedral, 22 February 1947. The picture includes, left to right: Tommy Daniels, Harry Inglis and Robert Scott from Bearpark Colliery. The memorial is in black Spanish mahogany and was designed by Donald McIntyre. Originally it was a fireplace in Ramside Hall, Carrville, to the east of the city and was given by the Pemberton family.

Three lamp boys from Sherburn Colliery, *c.* 1910, including, on the right, a member of the Blacklock family whose address was 24 Dragon Villa, Sherburn Road. The average age of lamp boys was fourteen.

Men working on the old A1 road near Farewell Hall, *c.* 1938.

The building of Durham School Chapel, 1926. The chapel was built as a memorial to Dunelmians who had been killed in the First World War and was dedicated on 30 September 1926. A former pupil, killed on the first day of the Somme campaign, 1 July 1916, was the poet William Noel Hodgson of the 9th Devonshire Regiment. He had attended the school from 1905 to 1911. The chapel's architect and designer was Mr Brierley of Messrs Brierley and Rutherford of York. The contract work was carried out by Messrs Rudd and Son of Grantham.

7

The Built Environment

Bakehouse Lane, Gilesgate, c. 1933. This lane marked the boundary of St Giles' parish. To the right is what was the General Gordon public house, 63 Claypath. The lane became known as Kepier Terrace and reverted to Bakehouse Lane in recent times. The lane originally led to the communal bakehouse.

Sherburn Road Ends, *c.* 1904. To the right is the Queen's Head public house and on the left is what was known locally as the Store Corner. The property on the left stood on an ancient site known as the Maidens Bower. St Giles' Church records of 1629 show various entries for repairs to the Maidens Bower, which was described in 1860 as 'an enclosure used by the servant maids of Durham for milking their cows'.

The Duckpond, Gilesgate, *c.* 1947. The earliest reference to the Duckpond is 1584, when Rycharde Robinson was paid for scouring the Ducke Poole. The public health report of 1849 advises that the Duckpond be filled in and a water trough placed nearby for animals. The water trough still survives at the top of Gilesgate Bank.

Gilesgate Bank, *c.* 1910, looking towards the city. The 'dry bridge' can be seen in the centre; this was removed in 1923. Most of the property was demolished in the 1960s.

Woodbine Cottage which stood near Baths Bridge. On the left is the exit of Tinklers Lane (St Giles' parish boundary). The small sweet-shop can be seen at the bottom of the lane. Woodbine Cottage was a Georgian building that had to be demolished because of a landslide from the new Leazes Road. This photograph shows the occupants leaving on a cold November day in 1965.

Looking down Ravensworth Terrace, Gilesgate, c. 1946. The buildings on the left were removed to make way for the new Leazes Road.

Kepier Mill, gatehouse and the manor house of the Heaths, *c.* 1880. The mill was destroyed by fire on 24 September 1870 when the miller's son fell asleep and forgot to fill the hopper with corn. The gatehouse was built by Bishop Richard de Bury (1333–45). The manor house of the Heaths was built in the late sixteenth century. The house later became the White Bear Inn and in its final years the Kepier Inn; sadly it was demolished in 1892.

The restoration of Prebends' Bridge, Durham City, *c.* 1955. The earlier bridge was swept away in the great flood of 1771. The present bridge was built by George Nicholson, the cathedral mason, in 1772.

Prebends' Cottage, which stands on the south side of Prebends' Bridge, *c.* 1900. The cottage has changed very little over the last hundred years; it is the property of the dean and chapter.

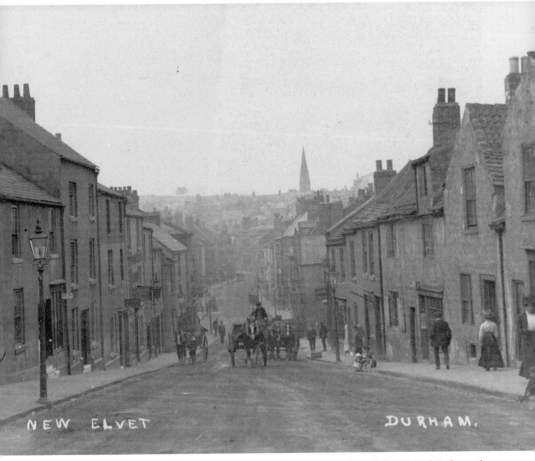

Looking down New Elvet, *c.* 1900. The spire in the centre is that of the United Reformed Church, Claypath. The Hare and Hounds public house stands to the left. All of the property in this picture was demolished to make way for Durham University's Elvet Riverside and Dunelm House. Small retail shops now occupy the right-hand side.

The first Baths Bridge, *c.* 1875. It was built in 1855 by public subscription, organized by Mr Edward Peele, who had a veterinary business in the city. The bridge provided a convenient crossing, linking Elvet to Gilesgate. The wooden bridge was replaced in 1894 by the iron bridge, which in turn was removed in 1962.

The removal in 1962 of the second Baths Bridge, built in 1894 at a cost of £700. The public baths stand to the right. The new concrete structure is very similar to the first bridge of 1855.

South side of St Giles' Church, *c.* 1830, drawn by William Pearson. The south aisle was added during the restoration of the church, 1873–6. In May 1894, while workmen were laying the new chancel floor, the vault was opened and examined. A number of coffins were found, belonging to the Heath family of Kepier. The vault was measured and resealed.

St Giles' Church from the lane which leads to Pelaw Wood, *c.* 1947. In March 1916 a poem about the ghost of St Giles' Churchyard appeared in the *Durham Advertiser*. The ghost was reputed to have been seen travelling down this lane in the direction of the ancient Holy Well which stood near the Silver Link Footbridge in Pelaw Wood.

Durham Observatory, *c.* 1840. The building was designed by Salvin and erected around 1840 by private subscription. An observer lived in the purpose-built house and worked under the direction of the Revd Temple Chevallier. In the first volume of his *History of Durham*, published in 1860, Fordyce records that Durham had the only established astronomical observatory between London and Edinburgh.

The obelisk which stands 100 ft high near Obelisk Lane, Western Hill, in the grounds of St Leonard's School, *c.* 1969. The obelisk was erected by W.L. Wharton of Dryburn Hall in 1850 at his own expense. He gave it to the observatory to use as a landmark to sight the observatory telescope. It marks the meridian 1,200 yd north.

The statue of the 3rd Marquess of Londonderry in Hussars uniform, *c*. 1925. This fine electroplated statue was unveiled on 2 December 1861. The sculptor was Raffaelle Monti (1818–81), a Milanese who came to England in 1848 and lived here until his death. This statue is considered to be his finest work. To the left of the statue is the city fire ladder and the railings belonging to the gents' underground toilets.

Kingsgate Bridge, looking towards Elvet, 1963. The bridge was designed by the late Sir Ove Arup and was opened in December 1963. The £36,000 bridge was commissioned by Durham University to provide a route across the river from Elvet to the peninsula. Its design and construction provided a talking-point; two slender V-shaped supports and decks were built on rotating bases on opposite banks of the river and then swung round to meet in the middle, 60 ft above the water. In December 1993, thirty years after its construction, it was awarded a Mature Concrete Structure Award by the Concrete Society for its timeless quality and elegant design.

This photograph is a testimony to the days when winters were white. It was taken outside the Woodman Inn, Lower Gilesgate, in 1938. The snow-plough is fighting its way through a blizzard.

Property at the bottom of Gilesgate Bank, *c.* 1966, demolished in about 1967 to make way for the new roundabout. The Drill Hall can be seen in the centre. It was here in August 1904 that General William Booth, the Salvation Army leader, gave a public lecture to the people of Durham.

Gilesgate Church of England School, 1966. The school was opened in October 1874; it later became the Parish Hall and Sunday School. During the last war it was used as a first-aid post. In its later years it became neglected and was demolished to make way for St Giles' Filling Station.

Gilesgate Moor, 1929. The Rex Cinema stands to the centre right of the picture. This was opened in 1930 by local grocer George Lamb. Before the local Catholic church was built it was used on Sundays for mass.

Elvet Bridge, *c.* 1900, showing the Paradise Lane area behind the present-day boat house. The chimney in the centre is that of Chisman's Iron and Brass Foundry.

Ivy Cottage, which stood near Brown's Boat House at the bottom of Paradise Lane, *c.* 1921. Because of its location it was often subjected to flood damage; it was also reputed to have had a ghost. The house was demolished in the 1960s to make way for the new road system and for the new Elvet Bridge.

A romantic view of Kepier from the Gilesgate goods line, *c.* 1933. The fields in the background are now part of Newton Hall Housing Estate which, when built in the '70s, was believed to be the largest private housing estate in Europe.

Steps leading to the gatehouse at Kepier, *c.* 1930. The old mangle is a reminder of the days when washing was an all-day chore which involved younger members of the family turning the handle on the mangle as the mother fed the washing through the rollers.

Shacklock Hall, *c.* 1840, home of the Henderson family who owned the carpet factory at Freemans Place. This house had previously been a farm and stood near the factory. The incident in the engraving is from William Henderson's *Notes and Reminiscences of My Life as an Angler* (1876), and involves the family cat.

North Road, *c.* 1900. It was constructed in 1831 to improve the Great North Road. Before this date the main route to the north was the old street of Framwellgate.

The Market Place in 1830, showing the old St Nicholas' Church, which was taken down in June 1857. Standing to the left of the church is the town house of the Nevilles; this was replaced by the new town hall, built in 1850 and officially opened on 29 January 1851.

St Nicholas' Church, Durham City, *c.* 1978. The church was refurbished in 1980 by the vicar, the Revd Dr George Carey, Archbishop of Canterbury. It was rededicated by the Bishop of Durham on 23 October 1981.

St Giles' parish clerk's house, *c.* 1900, which stood two doors up from the Britannia Inn. This building is typical of the style associated with Durham City. Many properties like this were demolished in the 1920s and 1930s. The dormer windows, pantile roofs and stone tiles were very common; now only a handful survive.

Count's House, *c.* 1890. This was in fact a summerhouse belonging to a house in the South Bailey. It is commonly called the Count's House after the Polish Count Boruwlaski who lodged at the home of the Ebdons near Prebends' Bridge.

Looking towards the Old Elm Tree public house, 12 Crossgate, *c.* 1928. The property to the right of the Elm Tree was replaced with council flats in the 1960s (Grape Lane).

Market Place Mill, *c.* 1933. Durham Ice Rink now stands to the left of the photograph. The mill was commonly called Martin's Flour Mill after the owner.

8
Military Matters

Buglers of the 1st Battalion Durham Light Infantry playing on the balcony of the town hall in July 1960. The battalion had been involved in a recruiting campaign.

Soldiers from the 43rd North Durham Militia in undress uniform on the steps of Durham Castle, *c.* 1865. The local gentry acted as officers while volunteers for the rank and file had to be drawn by ballot. The main role of the militia was home defence and in a time of war they could take over coastal defences, thereby releasing regular soldiers for services overseas.

The Militia Barracks (Vane-Tempest Hall), *c.* 1947, as drawn by Norman Richley, who was curate at St Giles' Church. In April 1864 contracts were given for the building of the barracks: Mr R. Alan, mason; Mr Appleby (Barnard Castle), joiner; Mr Pearson, joiner; and Mr P. Rules, slater. The building was opened in 1865 for the 43rd North Durham Militia. By the early 1880s the building was empty. The city took over the barracks in 1884 and used them as a smallpox hospital. In 1892 the barracks were purchased by Lord Londonderry for the 2nd Durham Artillery Volunteers. Until the late '30s many military occupants passed through. In the last war the tower was used as a look-out post for the ARP wardens. It was here that the idea came to light for a community building. The Gilesgate Welfare Association was formed in 1947.

The 8th Durham Light Infantry Headquarters, *c.* 1966. The Drill Hall stood at the bottom of Gilesgate Bank near the site of the roundabout; it had to be demolished to make way for the new through road in 1967. The coat of arms above the entrance was saved and is now incorporated in the new Drill Hall building (TA Centre).

Men from the 2nd Durham Volunteer Artillery, who were based at the barracks (Vane-Tempest Hall), *c.* 1905. Robert Savage is to the left in the front row. Many of these men would have been from the city area, as the volunteers were weekend soldiers.

Private Alfred Savage (brother of Robert, above, and Jack, opposite), seen here, in 1912, proudly wearing his uniform of the 8th Durhams. Alf later went on to join the Royal Field Artillery in 1913. He was one of the first to be called to the front in August 1914.

Private Jack Savage from Gilesgate, *c.* 1916. Jack was in the Royal Field Artillery in the First World War. After the war Jack was never the same. The British Army expected men to come home and to get on with life, but the war had affected Jack badly. A page from his sister's diary records that he left home on 25 August 1922. Jack was never to be seen again by his family in Durham.

The band of the 8th Durhams, *c.* 1927. The original photograph is entitled 'Boys of the Old Brigade'. Back row, far right, is Herbert Richardson whose father was head gardener at St Hild's College. They lived in School House, which was attached to the college.

Territorials from the 8th Durhams leaving the Market Place for Palace Green, Coronation Day, 22 June 1911. The coronation of George V was a great occasion for the city; all the streets and premises were ablaze with flags and floral decorations.

The Boer War memorial, 24 October 1912. The occasion was the laying of the colours of the 1st, 2nd and 3rd Battalions Durham Light Infantry. The cross was erected in December 1905 in memory of the men of the Durham Light Infantry who had lost their lives in the South African War. The cross was designed by Mr C.G. Hodges of Hexham and sculpted by Mr G.W. Milburn of York.

Durham Officer Training Corps Contingent, Hatfield Hall, 3 May 1913. The procession is seen here walking to the main entrance from the main gates in the North Bailey. The occasion was the installation of the new chancellor, the Duke of Northumberland, His Grace Henry George Percy KG. In the procession is the Prime Minister, Herbert Henry Asquith, the Bishop of London and Earl Curzon.

3rd Northumbrian Brigade, Royal Field Artillery, Durham City Battery, 1914. The scene is Durham Market Place, and they were about to leave for France. Most of the men were recruited from the city and were based at the barracks in Gilesgate.

A group of servicemen in the garden of Ivy Cottage, which stood near Brown's Boat House, c. 1915. In the centre are Mr Joseph Pattison (without hat), his wife Janet and children, Thomas and Mary.

The Curtis family, 13 Claypath, c. 1916. Mrs Curtis is wearing a Northumberland Fusiliers shoulder badge and her son on the far right wears a cap badge in his lapel. The man of the household, Charles Curtis, was fighting in France. This type of photograph was common as copies would be sent to loved ones at the front. Back row, left to right: Alice, Mary, Elizabeth, Elsie, William and Charles. Front row: Elizabeth and Emma.

Durham City heroes, June 1917. Left to right: Pte. Mathew Hanley DLI, awarded the Military Medal for bravery on the Somme after carrying six wounded men to safety under heavy shell fire; Sgt. W.H. Smith DLI, awarded Military Medal for saving two comrades who were wounded and under heavy shell fire; L/Cpl. Richard Savage, 10th Royal Hussars, awarded the Distinguished Conduct Medal in October 1914, for saving two officers under heavy shell and rifle fire who were lying wounded in no man's land. The naval officer in the front row is unknown.

Anniversary Memorial Service, 1925. The 10th anniversary of the 8th Durham Light Infantry's first action in France, during the Second Battle of Ypres. The venue was the old Militia Barracks (now Vane-Tempest Hall), Gilesgate. Back row, left to right: Lieut. J. Bramwell, Lieut. Watson, Captain J.N.O. Rogers, Lieut. S. Platten MC, Captain T.A. Saint, Captain J.R. MacDonald MC, RAMC, Lieut. S. Aberdeen DCM, Lieut. Willis. Middle row: Captain J. Hornsby, Lieut. A. Rooney, MC, Lieut. Eltringham, Captain Harmer, Col. C. Lomax CF, Captain T.A. Bradford DSO, Captain G.E. Blackett, Captain J. Atkinson DCM, Captain T.F. Brass, Lieut. J.G. Raine MC, Captain H. Wilkinson MC, T.D, Lieut. Alderson, Lieut. E. Fisher. Front row: Captain E.A. Leybourne TD, Major E.H. Veitch MC, TD, Major J.A.S. Ritson DSO, MC, TD, Major J. Turnbull, TD, Colonel J. Turnbull, CMG, VD, Lieut.-Col. J.R. Ritson OBE, TD, Colonel W.C. Blackett CBE, TD, Captain H.A. Stenhouse, Captain W. Francis, Captain E.H. Motum, Captain R.A. Worswick.

The Northumberland Hussars, B Squadron (Territorials), 1928. The Hussars were a cavalry unit based at the barracks. Most of the men were local lads who joined to have some excitement at weekends. One regular exercise was tent-pegging; this was when mounted Hussars armed with lances would try to retrieve tent-pegs from the ground. Standing second from the right is Ambrose Savage.

St Cuthbert's Church Lads' Brigade, c. 1928. Back row, left to right: Billy Palmer, Henry Gibson, John Lee, Robbie Peel. Front row: Walter Robinson and Ronnie Modral. The brigade was run by Cecil Ferens, a solicitor, from Saddler Street.

An historic visit to Durham by the 1st Battalion, Durham Light Infantry, on Saturday 21 July 1934. The photograph was taken at Sherburn Road Ends, Gilesgate. The title of the photograph was 'Three cheers to the Mayor' (Councillor J.C. Fowler). After a short speech by the mayor they were entertained at the barracks.

St Giles' knitting circle, *c.* 1939, knitting for the troops. The photograph shows the strong community spirit that was built up in the early days of the Second World War.

Mrs Pragnell from Claypath, seen here collecting her ration of coal in 1943. This scene was quite common in the north of England until the 1950s. Coal delivery dates were an opportunity for youngsters to earn a penny or two for carrying the coal to their neighbours' coalhouses. The spire is that of the United Reformed Church.

Durham City Auxiliary Fire Brigade, seen here in the playing field of the Girls' Grammar School, Providence Row, 1940. The brigade was stationed nearby. The large chimney at the rear was the city incinerator, which stood in the ice rink car park.

Durham Auxiliary Fire Service, September 1940. Allergate station members are about to take part in a practice at Durham City Baths. The section officer in charge was Mr J. Dunn. Durham had the first ladies' crew in the north of England. In the background to the right is Woodbine Cottage.

The Post Office Home Guard Platoon, *c.* 1942. The photograph was taken at the rear of the old post office in Claypath. Exercises were held at Kepier Rifle Range; the platoon's arms consisted of one Thompson machine-gun and one .303 rifle. Back row, left to right: Ross Cunningham, -?-, -?-, A. Dunn, F. King, -?-, -?-, S. Jordan, H. Winter, -?-, T. Hardy. Middle row: H. Marley, F. Bateman, H. Mole, A. Lawson, H. Harris, N. Alison, J.F. Magee, G.A. Johnson, T. Herbert, P. Hart, D. Cook, H. McGregor. Front row: J. McClurg, S. Grant, G. Thompson, F. Spirit, C. Donaldson, T. Blythe, J. Ward, F. Benson, J. Wilson.

Durham City Air Training Corps, *c.* 1941. In the front row behind the cross is Ron Liddle from Pittington and behind him is Cecil Ferens, who was commanding officer. Meetings were held at Whinney Hill School. Many of the men went on to join the Royal Air Force.

9

Transport

London & North Eastern Railway bus service operating from Durham railway station, c. 1930. The bus is a Birmingham-built SOS 'S' type, normal control, 31-seater, bought by Northern General Transport in 1926.

Elvet station, *c.* 1948 (opened in 1893), which stood on the site now occupied by the Magistrates' Court. The station was the terminus of a short branch line which ran through Sherburn where it joined two other spurs, one to Whitwell Colliery and the other to Shincliffe. The station was closed to passengers in January 1931, but continued to carry Miners' Gala passengers each July until 1953. Between 1931 and 1949 it was used as a goods station. The station was sold to Durham County Council in 1949 and demolished in 1963.

An engine leaving Elvet station, *c.* 1949. Sherburn Road Estate can be seen on the left.

London & North Eastern Railway engine (LNER/BR Class 'J39' 0–6–0 locomotive) leaving the turntable at Elvet station, *c.* 1949, after working a Miners' Gala special. On the right is the water-tower used for filling the engines.

Horse-drawn prison van outside Durham railway station, 1906. Many older residents remember waiting for the 'Black Maria' to come down from the station with the policeman riding on the back.

Gilesgate goods station as seen from the old Engine Bridge, 1966. This was the first passenger station in the city and had opened in June 1844. The goods station was closed on 7 November 1966 under the Beeching plan. Beyond, to the right of this picture, was Kipling's coal yard.

Durham station including the engine sheds, c. 1958. The area is now a large car park for the station.

Belmont Viaduct, which linked Belmont to Brasside, *c.* 1933. This viaduct had been opened in 1856. It was one of the loftiest bridges of its kind in the kingdom. It stretched across the Wear at a height of 130 ft. The piers stand on stone which was brought from the Roman quarry at Rudchester, Northumberland.

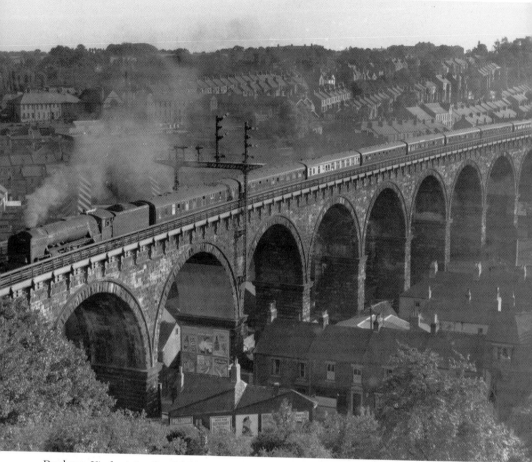

Durham Viaduct in the 1950s. Designed by the North Eastern Railway contractor Mr R. Cail, the viaduct had opened in 1857. It is 832 ft long and nearly 100 ft high, and has eleven arches. During its construction there were great problems with the foundations; long oak piles were driven by steam-power through peat moss and quicksand. The spaces between the piles were then filled with concrete; all together 21,300 ft of piling was used, as well as 184,500 cu ft of ashlar, 56,000 cu ft of brickwork, 140,000 cu ft of rubble and 142,000 cu ft of dry filling.

Mr J.W. Blackburn, 50 Dragon Villa, Sherburn Road, *c.* 1892. The cart was specially designed to transport Anglo-American lamp oil.

Blackburn's Cab Hire from Dragon Villa outside Woodlands and Caselaw on Gilesgate Green, *c.* 1900.

Durham bus station, *c.* 1958. St Godric's Church stands proudly in the background. The station was completed in 1929 on the site of what was R.V. Hill's flour mill. The old station was taken down in the 1970s and is now at Beamish Open Air Museum, awaiting re-erection.

Express bus which operated from the Market Place to Murton, *c.* 1927. The Express Service Omnibus Company was started by Mr William Showler in the early 1920s. The depot was at Gilesgate Moor opposite the Travellers' Rest public house.

The chief constable's car, a Daimler 10 hp, *c.* 1929, at the rear of the old police station, Elvet.

Temporary Police Constable Fred Forbes (left), *c.* 1928. Fred was from Whinney Hill and started as a TPC in 1926 during the General Strike. He worked with Durham Police Force until retirement in 1960. The van shown here was the new motorized 'Black Maria' used to transport prisoners. The body was built by Fred Forbes on a Lancia chassis.

Wood & Watson's wagon fleet, *c.* 1936. This photograph was taken in the barracks field, now Wood & Watson's car park. The wagons advertise a new drink, Watcheer. Wood and Watson's, 132 Gilesgate, were Durham's longest surviving mineral water manufacturers, established in about 1890. The founder, William Henry Wood, was mayor of the city in 1909 and 1919. He had come to Durham from Bedlington Colliery, Northumberland, where his family owned Wood & Sons Ltd, mineral water manufacturers. Initially he had premises near the County Hospital, before moving to Gilesgate around 1894. The trade mark of the factory has always been Durham Cathedral. Their stone ginger-beer bottles are now very rare and are collectors' items.

Silver Street at its narrowest point, *c.* 1965. Until 1967 this road was the main route through the city centre. The bus is a United Bristol 'LS' type, servicing Durham to Peterlee.

A lucky escape for the driver of this car, which was sandwiched between two buses on Gilesgate Bank, *c.* 1968.

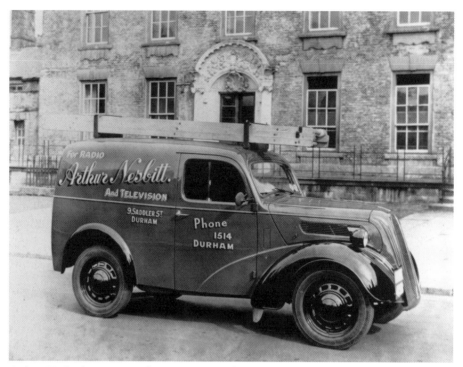

Arthur Nesbitt's van on Palace Green outside Cosins Hall, 1953. Arthur Nesbitt ran a radio and television service on Elvet Bridge opposite Magdalene Steps.

Traffic congestion, Elvet Bridge, *c.* 1970. The bridge was restricted to pedestrians only in the early 1970s.

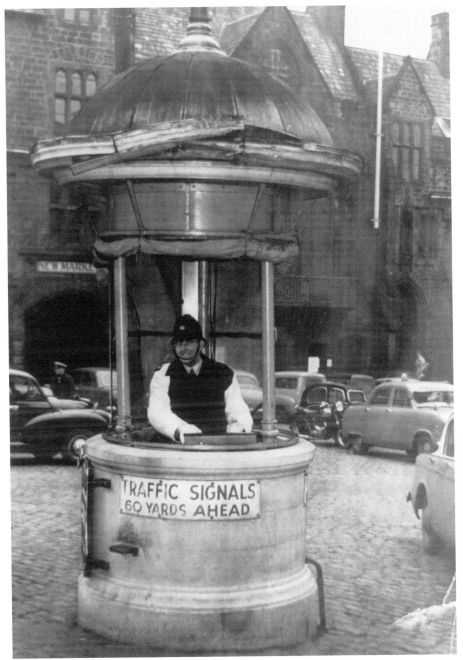

Durham's first police box, *c.* 1955, used for directing traffic through the Market Place. This was the first of its kind in the country. The man in the box is PC Tommy Stephenson.

The naming of the *Durham Light Infantry* steam engine, April 1958. The ceremony took place at Durham station in the presence of Mr T.H. Summerson, chairman of British Rail, and Col. K.M. Leather, who commanded the Light Infantry brigade.

Acknowledgements

So many people have donated photographs to the Gilesgate Archive that it is impossible to thank them individually. Institutions which have helped include:

Durham University Library, Palace Green • Durham City Reference Library
Durham Arts, Libraries & Museums Department, Durham County Council
the Taylor Collection • the Armstrong Trust • the trustees of the
Durham Light Infantry Museum & Mr I. Forsyth

Without this assistance this book would never have been possible and the authors acknowledge it gratefully. If any reader has new material or information, it would be helpful if contact was made with: **Mr Michael Richardson, 128 Gilesgate, Durham DH1 1QG (0191-384-1427).**

Part Two
Durham at Work

*Mrs Elizabeth Eltringham from the Queen's
Head Yard, Back Silver Street, c. 1932.
She is seen here doing the family washing
with her poss-stick and tub. A reminder of the
good old days!*

Introduction

The city and diocese of Durham chose 1995 to celebrate the millennium of their foundation because it is 1,000 years since the monks from Lindisfarne brought the body of St Cuthbert to Durham. We know, however, that there was a Roman settlement at Old Durham and an ancient hill fort at Maiden Castle, just outside the modern city.

Today the city of Durham is increasingly concerned with ecclesiastical and educational matters. The buildings round Palace Green – the Norman castle and the Romanesque cathedral at opposite sides – were declared a World Heritage site by UNESCO in 1987. The university, founded in 1832 by Bishop Van Mildert – the last of the Prince Bishops – is expanding, with a college at Stockton, and special relations with Teikyo University in Japan.

At the time of the beginning of photography, the city had just acquired a main line railway and a remarkable viaduct, of which an unusual early picture is included in this book. An achievement of Victorian engineering often underrated, the viaduct deployed some 21,300 ft of oak pilings, for it was built on sand, yet had a span of 832 ft. It is from the viaduct, built in 1855–7, that most people have their first view of Durham City, set in the hollow below, within the famous loop of the River Wear.

The population of 14,088 recorded in the 1851 census – just over half that of the city today – included 898 Irish people, almost all brought to the north-east by employment on the construction of the railways. Ten years before, the census showed the existence of 913 domestic servants in a population of 13,188, an indication of the middle-class nature of the city. In 1851, as many as 308 people had jobs in agriculture, for the city retained close connections with its rural hinterland, as several of Michael Richardson's photographs demonstrate; I particularly like the picture of the farm hind (see page 187).

The two main industries within Durham City in the late nineteenth and twentieth centuries were carpet weaving and organ building. There were in the city itself several coalmines, none large, and from 1871 Durham was the scene of the Miners' Gala, which became world famous. Coalmining, however, was a major occupation of the county rather than of the city. In 1851, 201 males and 32 females were involved in carpet weaving, a seventh of them children under the age of fourteen. The weavers, many of whom had come in from other weaving districts, lived mostly in Back Lane, to the north of St Nicholas' Church which dominates Durham's Market Place. The carpet factory by the River Wear dated from 1814, and was known as Henderson's under three generations of that family until its sale to Crossleys of Halifax in 1903, with the loss of over 300 jobs. Fortunately, a workman at the factory leased buildings and machinery from the Hendersons, and rebuilt the factory's fortunes as Hugh Mackay's. The resulting company received the Royal Warrant in 1972, three years after an arson attack destroyed the works and caused the removal to a site at Dragonville on the eastern outskirts of the city.

Harrison & Harrison Ltd, organ builders, began only in 1872 when the Revd Dr J.B. Dykes persuaded Thomas Harrison to remove from Rochdale; Thomas was shortly joined by his brother James. An old paper mill, in what is now Hawthorn Terrace, was purchased, and this was enlarged; the business is still conducted on the same site. Harrison organs are to be found all over the world, in cathedrals especially; the firm has an enviable reputation for restoring historic organs, including its own earlier models.

The most important industrial establishment in the neighbourhood of Durham in about 1900, however, was the Grange Iron Co. which leased the site of Grange Colliery at Carrville, just over two miles from the city centre, from the Marquis of Londonderry in 1866. The works covered some ten acres and constituted a township in their own right, for dwellings were created for the considerable workforce. In 1887 the company was awarded two silver medals and a bronze at the Royal Exhibition at Newcastle for compound air-compressing engines, air locomotives for underground haulage, and for colliery jigging screens. Its products were regularly exported.

Michael Richardson's photographs are rich in business interest. One of the Durham families long established in local enterprises was the Colpitts family. The grandfather ran stagecoaches with his brothers between Durham and Newcastle and Durham and Sunderland. The father opened the City Hotel in 1883. The brothers T. and H.C. Colpitts owned the Criterion Hotel from 1899. This was a favourite rendezvous for sportsmen, specializing in a blend of Scotch whisky in two strengths. J. and G. Archibald, owners of iron stores in Sunderland, in 1910 bought the business of T.J. Tomlinsons. Founded in 1840, the business had moved to a large warehouse at Gilesgate goods station in 1884. The Archibalds gave their name to a business with much more diversification in building materials when they sold to William McIntyre in 1924; the firm, greatly changed though it is, still flourishes. One of the more noticeable buildings in the city with a tall chimney, at the junction of Atherton Street and North Road, was used at the end of the nineteenth century as the premises of Geo. Hauxwell and Sons, Iron and Brass Founders. Many drain covers and grates in the city bear the name to this day.

Michael Richardson's photographs recall for us a variety of tradesmen and professionals, such as the Edis family of photographers; Joseph Brown the boat builder (Durham is the northern home of the modern racing-boat); the Gradon family of builders and timber merchants who produced two mayors of the city in 1875 and 1916; the Goodyears, who had one of the largest building and contracting businesses in the north-east (F.W. Goodyear was mayor twice, in 1916 and 1926); the McCartans, father and son, who were linen manufacturers and merchants in Gilesgate and had a branch in Dromara, Co. Down; and Ralph Charlton, wholesale and retail draper of Claypath, who had spacious showrooms and millinery workrooms on the premises.

One of the rarer pictures shows Sherburn Hospital Chapel after the disastrous fire of 1864. Another evocative photograph is of Christmas Day at the Union Workhouse, later St Margaret's Hospital. Life in Durham was often not easy for young or old. Walter Shea, who spent his life in the service of Mackay's, has recorded his early days: 'Times were really hard; the school leaving age was fourteen but lots of children started work long before that, usually working nights, Saturdays and school holidays, as delivery boys. I started work as a delivery boy for a butcher in Claypath. I worked about one hour in the morning before school then an hour or so after school, and all day on Saturday, for which I was paid 2s 6d. This was in 1916. My father, who was a weaver at Hugh Mackay's, seldom had a full week's work, except at certain times of the year.'

Even people in full employment in the north-east received relatively low wages. In 1877 the staff of Harrison & Harrison, twenty-three of them, enjoyed total wages of £33 12s 8d per week; craftsmen earned only between £1 7s and £2 10s 6d. In 1901, the wages bill at the organ-makers for fifty-six staff was still only £104 3s ½d. Arthur and Harry Harrison, who ran the business, drew only £3 each a week and their retired father £10. Nationally, wages were some 80 per cent higher in 1900 than in 1860 and living standards had improved, though in many areas – including Durham – not housing conditions. Wages were comparatively static between the world wars, and real economic improvement came only after 1939. Moreover, unemployment was an endemic feature of north-east life for whole generations.

Everyone will find something in this book which will intrigue them about the past in an area which arouses such loyalty in its people. For some, the photographs will be reminders of good old days; for others a record of past suffering. All will feel a debt to Michael Richardson and those who have contributed their photographs to his collection for stirring up memories, whether glad or sad.

Professor G.R. Batho
University of Durham

10
Businesses

Aitchisons grocer's shop, 1 Alexandria Crescent, c. 1905. The shop was later run by Mr T. Robertson. More recently the property has been used by Durham School.

John Reed Edis, the famous Durham photographer, photographed by his daughter Daisy, *c.* 1937. John Edis was born at Tottenham Court Road in 1861 and was proud of the fact that he was a Londoner. After training at the newly formed London Polytechnic he worked with his uncle, who had a photography business in the Strand. He then came north in 1883 and worked at Darlington, where he married, before moving to Durham in 1890. There he joined Fred Morgan. He soon branched out for himself, first at 27 Sherburn Road and later at 53 Saddler Street, moving to 52 Saddler Street *c.* 1898. During the First World War John served as a special constable in the city.

Daisy Edis photographed by her father,
c. 1903. Daisy started working with her
father at the age of fifteen. She went on
to become an artist in her own right,
her portraits being exhibited as far away
as Japan and America. She married
George Spence, but continued to use her
maiden name until she died in 1964.
She is buried in St Giles' 1927
churchyard.

Daisy's son, John Edis Spence,
photographed by Daisy in about
1927. This portrait was exhibited at
the International Exhibition at Ohio,
USA in 1933, and was titled 'My
Son'. It won an Award of Merit. John
became a naval chaplain and later an
Honorary Canon of Truro Cathedral.

Mary Wilkinson in period costume, an
exhibition photograph by Daisy Edis,
1920s. Mary was a re-toucher for
Edis's all her working life.

The Edis Studio, 52 Saddler Street, 1920s. These premises are now the offices for the
British School of Motoring. John Edis opened the studio here in about 1898. The
premises had previously belonged to a Miss Brewster, who was listed as a fancy hair-
worker in *The Durham Directory* of 1897.

Harrington's mobile kitchen at the top of Station Lane, 1890s. Joseph Harrington, pictured in the centre, was a shoe and clogmaker of 181 Gilesgate. He sold takeaway food from his mobile kitchen in the evenings in Durham Market Place.

Harrington's Tea Tent on the Racecourse for the Miners' Gala, 1890s.

Miss Emma Jarvis outside her tobacconist's shop, 2 Old Elvet, June 1911. The shop was decorated for the coronation of King George and Queen Mary. This is one of four identical shops which were built in about 1905. The site had previously been that of the Durham City Working Men's Club, originally the Wheatsheaf Inn (see page 223).

The corner of Old Elvet showing 1 Old Elvet, which was Hayton's newsagents, *c.* 1910. The property is now an off-licence. The properties to the left of Hayton's are the four small retail shops which replaced the Durham City Working Men's Club.

Durham County Hospital, August 1933. The hospital was built in about 1849–50 at a cost of £7,518 14*s* 10*d*, in the Elizabethan style. Much of the old building still survives, but has been hidden by modern extensions. It is now a psychiatric hospital.

Christmas Day at the workhouse, Crossgate, *c.* 1924. The workhouse was built in 1837, and was known as the Union Workhouse. When built it contained ten rooms as sleeping apartments and a dining hall, which also served as a chapel. The workhouse was capable of containing 150 inmates. It is now a nursing home and student accommodation for St John's College after many years as St Margaret's Geriatric Hospital.

Old Durham Fever Hospital, *c.* 1918. The hospital was situated near the site of the old Shincliffe Mill, now part of the Shincliffe Mill Boarding Kennels. The hospital was erected in 1910. Back row, second from the left, is Matthew Clarkson. The isolation period was approximately six weeks.

Ramsbottom's pork butchers, 106 Claypath, *c.* 1910. The shop stood below what is now Boots the Chemists opposite St Nicholas' Church. It later became Fred Robinson's (see below).

Fred Robinson's pork butchers, 106 Claypath, *c.* 1954. The shop was demolished in the 1960s. Miss Jean Reed is seen standing in the doorway. To the left of the shop was the King's Arms Hotel.

Samuel Hume, jeweller and clock maker, 17 Elvet Bridge, *c.* 1890. Samuel originated from Glanton, Northumberland, and first started business in Houghton-le-Spring before coming to Gilesgate in 1861. He later moved to the premises of the late John Crudas & Son, 17 Elvet Bridge. He died in 1909, and the business was carried on by his son-in-law Walter Holdsworth until 1923, when the business moved to 1 North Road.

S. Hume, jeweller, 1 North Road, *c.* 1923. Walter Holdsworth (on the left) with George R. Middlemass, a watch and clock repairer in his employ. The shop became Alexander's around 1927, and later it was called In Time. The building is now demolished, the Halifax Building society occupies the site.

Mr W.A. Bramwell, jeweller, 24 Elvet Bridge, *c.* 1929. Mr Bramwell was a keen photographer and a member of Durham City Camera Club; it is thanks to him that many scenes from Durham's past have been preserved. Many of the slides the late Dr Gibby (1902–89) used for his well-loved talks on Durham history were originally taken by Mr Bramwell.

The Eclipse wallpaper shop, 9 Saddler Street, *c.* 1929. The shop stood opposite Magdalene Steps.

Maynards Ltd, confectioners, 8 Saddler Street, 1929. The shop window display is for the Miners' Gala. Maynards had a number of shops in the city. The girl on the right is Grace Adams.

Mrs Hughes, 38 Gilesgate, Durham's last straw mattress maker, *c.* 1920. The property stood to the left of the old Drill Hall at the bottom of Gilesgate Bank.

Mr Robert Burns Wilkinson pictured on the right, with his nephew George Elgey, outside the general dealers' shop which he ran with his wife. It stood at the bottom of Gilesgate Bank left of Moody's Buildings, in the 1930s (see page 170 for a photograph of Mrs Wilkinson, his wife).

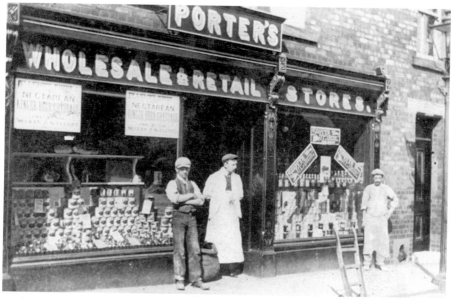

Porter's Stores, 43 Gilesgate, c. 1910. Standing in the doorway is Joseph Francis Porter. Porter's was an old-established firm which started up in about 1861. It also had a shop in North Road, where the electricity showrooms are now. The premises at Gilesgate stood to the right of the old Drill Hall and were later used by Cowies' Motor Cycles as a showroom. They were demolished in about 1967 for the new through road and Gilesgate roundabout.

Robert J. Maddison, general dealers, 201 Gilesgate, c. 1890. The photograph was taken by Obadiah Woodcock, a photographer from 193 Gilesgate. The shop is now a private house, and stands approximately opposite the Woodman Inn, Gilesgate.

A group of painters pictured in Durham Indoor Market, in the early 1900s. On the right of the front row is Isaac Arckless from 2 Wanless Terrace. The photograph shows some of the butchers' stands in the background with the hooks for hanging meat.

Lockerbie's shoeing forge, 111 Gilesgate, *c.* 1904. The forge stood behind the old Bay Horse public house, now rebuilt and called the Durham Light Infantryman.

Ice-cream carts belonging to the Dimambro family, *c.* 1911. The building on the left is part of Maynards Row. This area was demolished in the late 1940s to make the new entrance for the Gilesgate Community Centre (Vane Tempest Hall).

Durham City postmen, 1920s. The uniforms have an American Civil War look about them. The old post office stood in Saddler Street. The post office moved to Claypath in 1929 and, more recently, to Albert House, Silver Street.

Builders working on the construction of the Cottage Homes, Crossgate Moor, built by Ainsley Brothers of Durham, 1926. On the far right of the front row, standing, is Fred Hinsley. The Cottage Homes were officially opened by the Durham Board of Guardians on 26 March 1927. They now belong to the Durham Johnston Comprehensive School.

The founder of Wood & Watson's Mineral Water Works, William Henry Wood, pictured when he was Mayor of the City, 1919. He was also Mayor in 1909. A well- known Freemason, William Wood died in 1924 and a fine granite tombstone marks his grave in St Giles' 1870 churchyard. The business of W.H. Wood was established in about 1890, and he was later joined by Mr Joseph Watson, his brother-in-law. Mr Watson retired from the partnership just before the start of the First World War.

The old office of Wood & Watson's Ltd, 132 Gilesgate, *c.* 1960. The site previously belonged to Child's Tannery. The building was demolished and rebuilt in about 1960. To the left of the photograph is the lane leading down to the Silver Link footbridge and Pelaw Woods. Now demolished, a house has been built on the site of the office.

The loading bay for the wagons at Wood & Watson's, November 1947. This photograph shows the new bottle crates, which were bakelite and aluminium. These were not successful and the firm soon reverted to using the old-fashioned wooden crates. Standing on the wagon is Vic Richardson, one of the drivers.

Half of the staff from the Durham City Provincial Laundry, Providence Row, 1937. Back row, left to right: Nelly Crossman, Joan Egan, Kitty Burns, Hilda Robinson, Gladys Soulsby, Florrie Pattison. Middle row: Mary Shiell, Margaret Mortimer, Olive Akenhead, Ethel Whale, Violet Wills, Nora Stainsley, Peggy Forster, Lydia Adamson, Thomasina Redden. Front row: Mary Cooper, Elsie Crow, Edith Brown, Doris West, Betty Proud, Rene Clark. Seated: Evelyn Bell, Nora Liddle.

Edwin Oliver, tobacconist, 82 North Road, *c.* 1920. The shop window advertises Procopides cigarettes, once a popular brand but now unknown.

R.A. Charlton, draper and milliner, 103 Claypath, 1913. Mr Ralph Charlton established the business in 1871 in conjunction with Messrs J. and R.A. Stokes; in 1884 the two Stokes retired, leaving Mr Charlton the sole proprietor. The instruments hanging above the windows reflected heat on customers looking in the shop windows.

William Rolling outside his fruit shop at 19a Sunderland Road near the present Edge Court, Gilesgate, *c.* 1933. Rolling later had a shop built on the opposite side of the road.

Johnson & Cosgrove, family grocers, 45 Gilesgate, 1935. The shop stood at the bottom of Gilesgate bank to the right of Station Lane. The premises had previously been William Bramley's fancy drapers. The property was demolished to make way for the new through road in about 1967.

John Oliver, fishmonger and curer, 131 Millburngate, *c.* 1950. The shop stood to the right of the Five Ways Inn, and is now Gregg's the bakers. The name John Oliver still survives at Oliver's shop, 57 Hawthorn Terrace, Durham City.

Mr John Oliver, the third generation of John Olivers serving in the fishmonger's shop, 131 Millburngate, *c.* 1950. The business was established in the 1880s. The previous shop stood over the road at 2 North Road.

Ballard's tobacconists, *c.* 1944. The shop stood to the right of Oliver's fishmongers, at 132 Millburngate. On the left is pictured Mrs Mary E. Ballard and on the right Carrie Coulson. The business later moved to the top of North Road.

The staff from Boots the Chemist, which also had a lending library, 29 Silver Street, 1947. The photograph was taken by Daisy Edis outside the almshouses on Palace Green.

Mr John Oliver (not of the same family as the fishmonger) with his fruit and vegetable cart at Teesdale Terrace, Gilesgate Moor, *c.* 1949. He is seen here selling bilberries to his sister, Mrs Elizabeth Brice.

Tommy Atkinson, the projectionist at the Rex Cinema, Gilesgate Moor, on the closing night, 18 January 1958. He is seen loading his last film, *The Eagle Squadron*, after sixteen years at the Rex. In that time he had seen almost five thousand films.

Mason's cash chemists, 69 Saddler Street, 1938. To the far left is Earl's the baker, famous for their pies, and to the right Harland's wet fish shop; the latter later became Macdonald's, and, in its final years, Peacock's. Waterstone's bookshop now occupies the site of the chemists. The ancient street name Fleshergate can be seen above the doorway on the extreme right of the picture.

Joseph William Pattison standing in the city's electric power station, *c.* 1897. Joseph went on to serve in the First World War (see page 237).

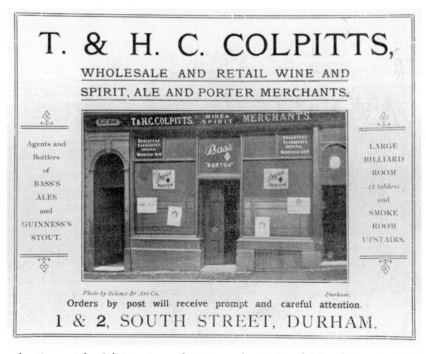

An advertisement for Colpitts wine and spirit merchants, 1 and 2 South Street, *c.* 1909.

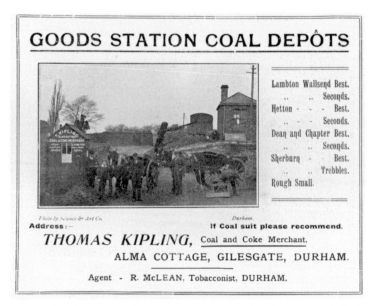

Kipling's coal yard, Gilesgate goods station, *c.* 1909. Kipling's was established in about 1889, and was one of the main suppliers of household coal to the city. Many residents will remember going to Kipling's coal yard where one could buy as little as a bucket of coal if there was a cash flow problem.

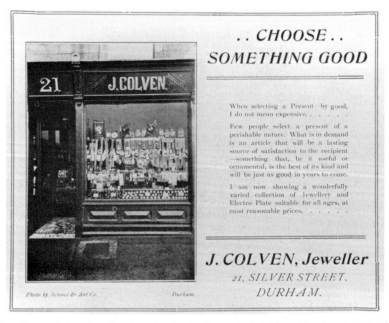

An advertisement showing the shop-front of J. Colven's, 21 Silver Street, *c.* 1909. The site is now a pizza restaurant at the bottom of Silver Street.

An interesting advertisement showing the portrait of Thomas Newby, plumber and gas lighting engineer to the Dean and Chapter, 48 North Bailey, *c.* 1909. At this time his work was in great demand, as the main source of lighting was gas.

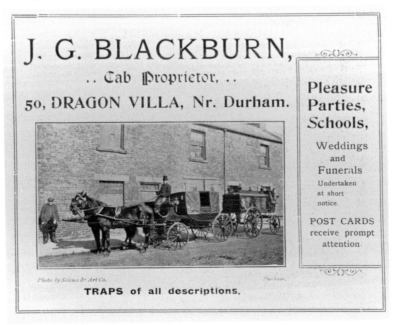

Blackburn's cab business, at Dragon Villa, *c.* 1909. On the right can be seen their horse-drawn hearse.

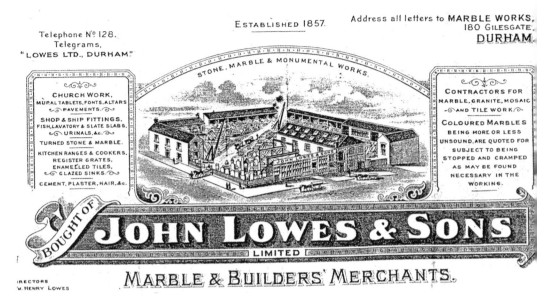

A letterhead belonging to John Lowes & Sons, marble & builders' merchants, 180 Gilesgate, from the 1920s. The marble works was founded by John Lowes in 1857. The premises had previously been a fine town house with its own orchard. Lowes soon became a well-respected firm, receiving orders from as far away as Exeter in the south and Frazerburgh in Scotland. At one time Lowes was the only works using Frosterley Marble and Wolsingham Blue.

Lowes Marble Works yard, *c.* 1910, showing the large cutting machine which was still in use when the works closed in the early 1960s.

Mr J.E. Hughes of Gilesgate with F.W. Goodyear's builders' van in their yard at the top of Claypath, on the left of the old General Gordon public house. Goodyear's started in about 1895. The old Palladium Cinema in Claypath and the Fighting Cocks public house, South Street, were built by this firm.

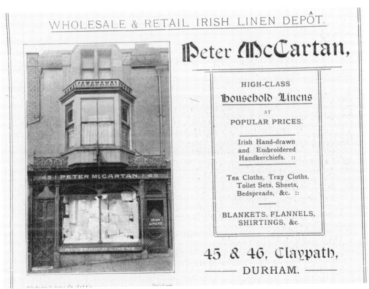

Peter McCartan's Irish Linen shop, 45 and 46 Claypath (now selling fishing tackle), *c.* 1909. Originally the business was established by Peter's father, Michael McCartan, in 1839.

Mr Bob Dickinson (with beard) at his bookstall in Durham Indoor Market, 1970s. Mr Dickinson retired from the indoor market in 1993. He specialized in antiquarian books and books of local interest. He was also a lecturer in Classics at Durham University.

Archibald's showroom, Jagal House, at the bottom of Gilesgate Bank, 1938. The building had previously been St Giles' church hall. In its final years, before it was demolished in the early 1960s, it was Cowie's motor cycle showroom, which Tom Cowie characteristically named Earls Court.

11
Transport

Mr Harry Spraggon, second from the left, stationmaster
at Sherburn House station, 1927. Mr Spraggon had
worked at Sherburn House station for fifty-four years.
He began his service in 1874 as a telegraph boy. His
father had been stationmaster before him; together they
rendered 106 years' service at Sherburn House station.
The locomotive standing in the station is a LNER Class
J27 freight engine.

Sherburn House station, showing the south-bound platform, in the 1890s. Lines branched off to Old Durham Colliery and linked up with Shincliffe station and later Elvet station in 1893.

Sherburn House station, north-bound platform, 1920s. The station, a wooden construction, stood between West Sherburn and Sherburn Hospital. It closed in 1931.

The building of the railway embankment for the city viaduct, *c.* 1855. The light building in the centre is the newly built Union Workhouse, which later became St Margaret's Hospital. The walled lane to the left is Red Hills Lane, which passes the Miners' Hall.

The viaduct under construction, seen from the top of North Road, *c.* 1856, showing the wooden scaffolding which was first erected.

Railway staff at Durham station, during the 1880s. The stationmaster was John George Wright; he is seen on the back row, left of the centre column.

Here we see three women porters at Durham station, *c.* 1918. They were taking the place of men who, during the First World War, had been called to the front. The lady in the centre of the back row is Janet Wilkinson, wife of Robert Burns Wilkinson (see page 147).

The opening of Sherburn Viaduct, 20 July 1844. The viaduct stood south of Sherburn Village near Sherburn House Hospital. Sherburn House Beck ran underneath it. Later the viaduct was turned into an embankment. The cathedral can be seen to the right of centre.

A Sunderland to Durham train crossing Brasside (or Belmont) Viaduct, c. 1915. The viaduct was opened in 1856. It is no longer in use, but still stands proudly linking Belmont to Brasside.

Belmont Junction, 1950s. The line on the right is leading off to Gilesgate goods station. It was here on 20 December 1921 that an express locomotive travelling from Aberdeen to Penzance with eleven coaches crashed into four standing coaches which were being shunted to a siding; fortunately no one was killed.

The Aberdeen to Penzance express locomotive Class Z 4–4–2 No. 720, lying on its side at Belmont Junction the day after the crash, 21 December 1921. Owing to alterations on the main line at Langley Bridge all rail traffic was diverted via Leamside.

The Hush Hush at Elvet station, Sunday 6 July 1930. The delight of every schoolboy, this type 4–6–4 locomotive was built at Darlington in 1929. It was the first of its kind, with a water-tube boiler patented by H.E. Yarrow and Nigel Gresley, the LNER's Chief Mechanical Engineer. Its appearance was described as a whale-like casing painted in battleship grey with stainless steel bands. Its registration number was 10,000.

Sherburn Hill Colliery engine 'Monty', 1959. Monty was an ex-War Department type 0–6–0 saddle tank. The locomotive worked the line between Sherburn Hill Colliery and Sherburn Village coal sidings. Monty became a well-known sight, especially with the children. He was painted in deep red. When Sherburn Hill Colliery closed in August 1965 he was transferred to Horden Colliery, where he was cut up in 1974.

The old engine sheds belonging to Shincliffe station, c. 1960. The station opened on 28 June 1839 and closed in 1893 when Elvet station was opened. It became a council depot, and in recent years the site has been transformed into private housing and renamed The Mews.

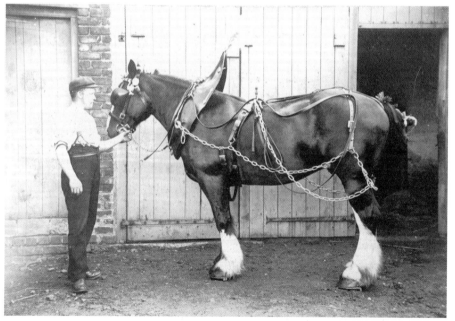

Mr John W. Blackburn with one of the heavy horses outside his father's stables at Dragon Villa during the 1890s (see page 163 for his father's business advertisement).

Mr Frank Fowler outside the stables at Wood & Watson's Ltd, Gilesgate, *c.* 1925. A terrible fire had occurred at the old stables on the night of 30 June 1901. Police Sergeant Hall and PC Robson were on duty at the Causeway Foot at the bottom of Gilesgate Bank, when they observed a red glow in the direction of W.H. Wood's Mineral Water Works. Upon reaching the site they discovered the stables on fire. They broke down the door and tried to rescue the horses. Out of the twenty horses stabled there twelve were saved. Damage was estimated at £600.

Mr George Rolling outside the Co-op Stables, behind the store at 7 Claypath, *c.* 1910. Mr Rolling was a driver with the store. He later set up in business by himself (see page 156 for a photograph of his first shop and his son William).

Mr R.W. Dixon, 81 Framwellgate, with his furniture removal wagon, early 1900s. In those days it was possible to move the whole household contents in one load.

The Durham Hand Laundry cart, of 60 Claypath, standing near the New Inn at the top of Church Street, *c.* 1912. Most of the work was from the middle classes in the city and from students at the university.

Wood & Watson's cart at Brancepeth village, standing outside the village school, *c*. 1925. Wood & Watson's delivered to all the mining villages on the outskirts of the city.

McKenzies, coal dealer and general carter, 77 Claypath, *c*. 1912. This horse and cart were entered in the Durham City Horse Parade at the Barracks, Vane Tempest Hall. The sacks on the cart probably contained household coal.

William Hockin, oil and egg merchant, from Surprise Cottage, Sherburn Road, *c.* 1910. This was a Horse Parade entrant at the Barracks. The trade constituted an odd combination – the oil would be lamp oil.

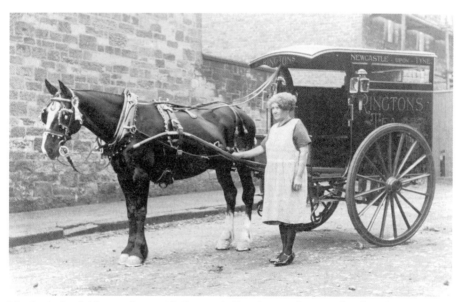

Mrs Jessie Layfield, seen here with Rington's Tea Cart at the top of Hallgarth Street near Mount Joy Crescent, *c.* 1929. Ringtons continues to be a household name in the region.

Norman Brown, photographed in the Bell's Ville area, Gilesgate Moor, with his cart advertising 'Light Carting Done', late 1940s. The building on the left is the rear of the old Hare & Hounds public house.

Joseph Johnson's 16 horsepower wagon from the City Brewery, 74 New Elvet, seen here outside the National Westminster Bank, Market Place, July 1916. The founder lived in Hallgarth Street from 1867 until 1884. The firm also had a branch at South Shields.

Missings' banana wagon from Station Lane, Gilesgate, dressed up for the Carnival Parade, *c.* 1923. It was quite common to find tropical spiders, occasionally alive, in their banana boxes. The young boys have their faces blacked; the driver is Sammy Burdon. The photograph was taken outside 129 Gilesgate at the Duck Pond (Gilesgate Green).

Mawson, Swan & Co., yeast and egg merchants, 115a Gilesgate, 1930s. The wagon fleet is seen here in the courtyard.

Fowler & Armstrong's garage, 74 New Elvet, *c.* 1926. In about 1921 Messrs W.A. Armstrong and M. Fowler, auctioneer and valuer, formed the business Fowler & Armstrong. They specialized in spare parts, and were the sole agents in the Durham area for Austin, Morris and Wolseley cars. In 1926 the firm purchased part of the disused premises of Joseph Johnson's brewery.

The new garage of Fowler & Armstrong, New Elvet, June 1952. The road on the right is Court Lane. In the 1980s the garage was demolished and in its place the Orchard House apartments were built.

A Durham District bus standing outside the Lord Seaham public house (now the Gilesgate Moor Hotel), Gilesgate Moor, *c.* 1953. The driver is Bill Merrington. Durham District took over the Express Omnibus Company in the early 1950s. The business was started by Mr W. Showler with one Ford car in the 1920s. The garage was at the top of Gilesgate Moor, opposite the Travellers Rest public house.

The Gillet and Baker bus, standing for a posed photograph in Waddington Street, *c.* 1954. The railway viaduct is seen in the top right-hand corner. Gillet & Baker had their garage at Quarrington Hill. The National Bus Company through its subsidiary United Automobile Services Ltd took over Gillet Brothers on 3 November 1974.

Mr Robert Inglis with a dual-purpose United Bus, during the early 1950s. The occasion was a student train-spotting day trip. Mr Inglis ended his working career at the GPO, Providence Row, Durham City, retiring in 1981 on health grounds.

A United bus standing in the old bus station at the top of North Road, May 1968. The station was built in about 1928 and was a cast-iron construction; it was taken down in 1976. The architect was A.H. Fennell and the contractor H.F. Mole, both from Chester-le-Street.

Gradon's lorry standing on Palace Green, c. 1946. The firm had its premises at 56 North Road. The business had been established in about 1814 by Forsters; Gradons took over in about 1840, as builders' merchants and monumental masons.

The building of the through road at the top of North Road, c. 1970. Here the bulldozer is seen cutting through to link up with the Millburngate Bridge.

The building of Millburngate Bridge and Millburngate House, 1966. The Millburngate Bridge was formally opened on 3 April 1967 by the Chairman of Durham County Council, Councillor S.C. Docking. The bridge was designed by Durham County Council's County Engineer and Surveyor, Mr H.B. Cotton, and County Architect Mr G.W. Gelson. The contractors were Holst & Co. Ltd. The cost of the bridge was £340,000.

The demolition of the second police-box in Durham Market Place, 18 November 1975. Its sole purpose was to direct traffic through the city centre by the manual operation of traffic lights. The police-box was a famous Durham landmark for many years (see page 240 for the first police-box).

Framwellgate Bridge, c. 1964. A swan narrowly avoids danger! It is hard to believe that before 1967 all vehicles, including the emergency services, travelled this route through the city. The bridge was pedestrianized in 1975.

12
Rural Scenes

Mr Thomas Turner, 1962. Farm hind at Bent House Farm, Dragonville, Mr Turner was awarded a long service medal for fifty years' service. A married farm-servant for whom a cottage was provided was called a hind in Scottish and north country dialects.

A charming rural scene in the 1920s; cows walking down Kepier Lane to the farmyard at Kepier. The farmer at the time was Robert Harper. Many older residents still refer to it as Harper's Farm.

A typical farmyard scene at Kepier, 1920s. The farmhouse is a much altered medieval building. The building covered in ivy to the right of the farmhouse in the orchard is possibly part of the medieval hospital buildings.

Kepier Gatehouse, photographed by John Edis, *c.* 1930. This gatehouse was built in about 1333–45 by Bishop Richard de Bury. The style is very similar to the College Gatehouse in the South Bailey.

Hallgarth Water Mill, 1920s. The mill stood on the roadside between Sherburn Village and Pittington. It was here on a hot summer Sunday on 8 August 1830 that Mary Ann Westhorpe, aged seventeen, was murdered by Thomas Clarke, nineteen. Clarke was tried and publicly executed at Durham in front of a crowd of approximately 15,000 spectators. On two other occasions tragedy hit the mill. Ex-police sergeant George Hugill suffered a fatal accident there in May 1923, when he was trapped in the cogs. His predecessor, the owner, was found drowned near the mill.

Shadforth Water Mill in the 1930s. The mill was originally known as Sherburn Mill East. It was a corn mill and was situated in a field called Ox Pasture. One of the earliest references to the mill is in 1605, when it was leased to William Shadforth for twenty-one years. The last occupants were the Crawford family, who left in the 1920s. The remains can still be seen as earthworks on the boundary between Shadforth and Sherburn.

Harvesting time at Bent House Farm, *c.* 1950. The men are seen here cutting hay at Dragon Ville. Left to right: Wilf Stoker, Thomas Turner and Bill Cowling. The field now has a supermarket built upon it. The building on the right was Fowler & Armstrong's garage.

Mr Gowland Collier with his haycart at the top of Church Street near the New Inn, *c.* 1910.

Sheep shearing at Old Durham Farm, May 1915.

Harvesting using the threshing machine at Lowes Barn Farm, c. 1920. The farmer at the time was W. Carter.

The Hallgarth Farm building in New Elvet, *c.* 1890. Originally the farm was called Elvet Hall Manor; most of the buildings were medieval. It was once part of the Priory estates and was administered by the hospitaller, the monk responsible for the Priory guests and their accommodation. The medieval tithe barn shown in the centre was threatened with demolition in the late 1960s, when the Prison Department of the Home Office wanted to demolish it to extend prison buildings. It is now the prison officers' club.

The old barn at Hallgarth Farm, 1920s. The buildings on the left were the business premises of A. Broughton, botanical brewer. The business was established in Durham by John Fentiman, son of a Yorkshire brewer, in about 1903. Mr Broughton became the proprietor in about 1908. Later the Fentimans and Broughtons became linked by marriage. The business closed in 1974.

Low Dryburn Farm, North End, *c.* 1920. The occupant at the time was Mr Edward Dixon, who was one of the directors of Pattison's cabinet-making and upholstery business, Elvet Bridge.

High Grange medieval tithe barn, *c.* 1960. It stood near where Gilesgate Junior School is now. This photograph was taken shortly before it was demolished to make way for the new housing estate. William Leech bought the High Grange Estate land from local farmer Mr W. Dixon in December 1959, for £17,537 10s. Many gardens on the High Grange estate salvaged stone for garden rockeries.

William H. Clarkson from Providence Place, Gilesgate Moor, with the milk-cart at Coldknuckles Farm, near Shadforth, *c.* 1906. (Coldknuckles Farm stood near Shadforth Mill – see page 190.)

Joseph March Clarkson with his niece, Mabel Clarkson, and great nephew John Myers, at Providence Place, Gilesgate Moor, about to set out to sell their home produce, *c.* 1914.

Farm labourers burying potatoes for winter storage at Houghall Farm, *c.* 1920. George Tennick is pictured third from the left.

St Cuthbert's Church, built in 1858 by E.R. Robson, seen from Wharton Park, *c.* 1935. The new County Hall building now stands to the right.

13
Education

A tree planting ceremony at Whinney Hill School, 1937. Left to right: Mr Thomas Pawson, Mr George Carpenter and the Marquess of Londonderry KG, Mayor of Durham.

Old Durham School, Dragon Villa, 1890s. The school had previously been a military barracks for the Marquess of Londonderry's 2nd Durham Artillery Volunteers. The school became a showroom and cottages named Vane Villas (Sherburn Road). They are now demolished.

A class from Old Durham School, *c.* 1898. Back row, second from the right, is Arthur Clarkson; centre row, second from the right, is Lucy Clarkson; and front row, right, are twins Isaac and Henry Clarkson.

Bede Model School – a classroom scene, *c.* 1900. The model school served as a practice school for the student teachers of Bede College. It closed on 31 August 1933.

Blue Coat Infants at Seaham Hall, 31 August 1911. The occasion was a summer fête given by Lord and Lady Londonderry for the Durham City schoolchildren. Three thousand children and their teachers left Elvet station on four different trains. Each child was presented with a commemorative medal portraying Lord and Lady Londonderry, Mayor and Mayoress of Durham, on one side and on the reverse 'Seaham Hall, August 1911'.

An aerial view showing Durham School, 1930s. To the left you can see St Margaret's allotments. In October 1988 all allotment holders received notice to vacate their plots from the agents acting for the diocese of Durham. It was later revealed that a developer was interested in the land for housing. A successful campaign was launched by the allotment holders to save them from the developers.

St Godric's Roman Catholic School, Castle Chare, 1928. One young boy in the front row is without shoes. This lack of adequate footwear was quite common in the late 1920s, as people were still suffering from the General Strike of 1926.

Teachers from Whinney Hill School, c. 1950.

Millburngate Nursery, early 1960s. This was built for the children of munition workers during the Second World War; the site is now occupied by Millburngate Shopping Centre.

Durham Castle (University College) as seen from the upstairs window of Smith the Chemist, Silver Street, *c.* 1936. This picture shows the view obtained when buildings were demolished for the construction of Marks & Spencer's new store. University College was the foundation college of the University of Durham.

St Mary's College, housed in The Cathedral College, *c.* 1921. The building is now The Chorister School. The college was dedicated to St Mary in 1920. The new St Mary's is situated off Quarry Heads Lane; the building was officially started in October 1947 when Princess Elizabeth (the present Queen) laid the foundation stone.

Hatfield Hall, North Bailey, *c.* 1910. Formerly an eighteenth-century coaching inn named the Red Lion, Hatfield became the second college of Durham University in 1846.

Teachers from St Joseph's Roman Catholic School, Mill Lane, Gilesgate Moor, 1963. Back row, left to right: T. Kain, K. Forrester, P. Doran. Front row: M. Dixon, P. Reed, T. Tobin, N. Watson, M. Doyle.

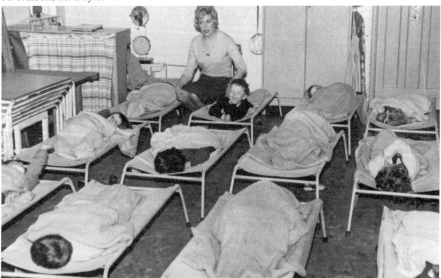

Sheila Rutherford watches over the children at Gilesgate Nursery, which stood near Wood & Watson's car park, *c*. 1965. The nursery established a much-valued afternoon sleeping period for the children. The nursery was similar to Millburngate Nursery (see page 202).

14

Industry

Two lamp boys from Framwellgate Colliery, 1919. On the left is Joseph Pallister, aged fourteen, from Smokey Row, Framwellgate Moor, photographed on his first day down the pit.

Men leaving the Grange Iron Works, Carrville, *c.* 1920. In 1887 at the Royal Exhibition at Newcastle upon Tyne the company was awarded two silver and one bronze medal for their colliery machinery. The iron works at Carrville closed in 1926 when it was amalgamated with Messrs J. Cook, Sons & Co. Ltd of the Washington Steel & Iron Works. The photographer was A. Dunn, South Street, West Rainton.

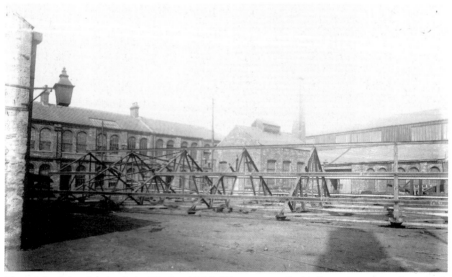

The yard of the Grange Iron Works, 1914. The iron works had its own gasworks, which produced all the lighting for the works and offices. Many of the buildings and bridges made were in kit form, with each part numbered. Photographs would be taken to help in the erection when the kit reached its destination.

The staff of the Grange Iron Works, *c.* 1916. At that time they were receiving orders from New South Wales, New Zealand, South Africa, China, Brazil, India and other parts of the world.

The turning shop of the Iron Works, 1890s. The Grange Colliery had previously occupied the site.

Kepier Colliery, *c.* 1850. The colliery was owned by Ralph Dixon of 64 Claypath. It was on the site of the present council yard at Glue Garth, Sunderland Road, Gilesgate. The colliery was well under way by 1818; it worked the Hutton & Low main seams. By 1870 the colliery was unproductive, and it was abandoned in 1872. Plans were drawn up by the city council in 1929 to turn the spoil heap into a play area, known locally as the 'Duff Heap'.

Sherburn Hill Colliery, 1920s. The chimneys on the right belonged to the coke works. The colliery was sunk in 1835, and was closed in August 1965.

Drift-mine workings in Kepier Wood, *c.* 1930. The coal tubs were pulled by steel ropes. The *Durham County Advertiser* of 6 July 1926 reported that John Smith, aged twenty-five, of Claypath, had been trapped by a fall of stone at Kepier Drift. There are still signs of mine-working in Kepier Woods, for example the small stone walls leading into the drifts from the towpaths.

Sherburn House Colliery, 1890s. It was sunk in 1844 and closed in 1932. The colliery was first leased to the Earl of Durham, later Lambton Collieries and later still Lambton and Hetton Collieries. In 1913 Sir B. Samuelson & Company took over the lease, and finally, in 1923, Dorman, Long & Co. The colliery site was opposite Grand View, Sherburn Village.

Miners from Sherburn House Colliery in the 1920s. Left to right: Robert Gainforth, Mr Ormiston and Sammy Bunch. Coal-hewers' wages were approximately 9s 8d per week in the 1920s.

Easington Public band in North Road for the Durham Big Meeting, 21 July 1951. Two months earlier (29 May), 83 men (including two rescue workers) from the colliery lost their lives in an explosion.

Brandon Colliery Prize Silver Band, 1929. The band had a high reputation and was under the direction of Fred Bowes as conductor. In 1934 they competed at the Crystal Palace Tournament. This photograph was taken outside the colliery manager's house.

A miner rests at the Racecourse on the afternoon of the Miners' Gala, *c.* 1950. Pelaw Wood is in the background.

A young boy, holding his bow and arrow, with his mother on the Racecourse at the Durham Miners' Gala, *c.* 1949.

A typical scene on Miners' Gala Day, 23 July 1938. Carters sell their wares. Again, the banners are draped in black.

Two miners from one of the colliery villages on the outskirts of the city exercising their dogs, 1930s. On the reverse of the picture the name Bill Routledge appears.

Mr Jack Wilkinson, left, working on an electrical motor at Messrs Hornes and Co., 67 New Elvet, c. 1948. The Durham branch was established in 1913 and specialized in repairing colliery machinery.

A young-looking Harold Wilson pays a visit to Bickley's Clothing factory, Dragon Ville, in the late 1940s.

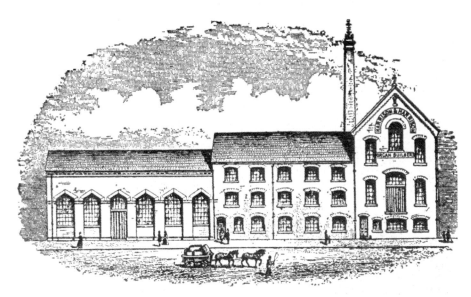

A nineteenth-century engraving of Harrison's organ factory in Hawthorn Terrace. The firm was founded by Thomas Hugh Harrison in Rochdale, Lancashire, in 1861. The factory site in Durham had previously been an old paper mill.

The workforce of Harrison's organ factory, photographed outside the main entrance for the firm's centenary (1861–1961).

Jack Ritchie, the district tuner, Harrison's organ factory, *c.* 1971.

Gilesgate Soap Works, 42 Gilesgate, 1880s. The Soap Works was established in October 1874 by the Co-operative Wholesale Society. Later, in 1902, the Drill Hall belonging to the 8th Durham Light Infantry was built on the site.

Old Durham Sand Quarry, 1930s. At the beginning of the Second World War a Roman bathhouse was discovered when the Durham City Sand & Gravel Company cut a test pit, with a view to extending the quarry. The Roman bathhouse was of the Antonine period; archaeological digs were carried out, but sadly the remains were lost for ever with the extensive quarrying.

William Coulson Fawcett, *c.* 1906. He was the last manager of Elvet Colliery. In 1906 he was lowered down a shaft, probably in the river banks, to inspect the flooded workings. His subsequent report led to the closure of the colliery and the loss of his job. He was the grandfather of William C. Fawcett, former headmaster of Cheveley Park Infant & Junior School, Belmont.

Hugh Mackay's stand at the North-East Coast Exhibition, 1929. This loom was worked by the Prince of Wales (later Edward VIII) when he visited the exhibition. The rug which was woven at the exhibition was later auctioned for the Durham Castle restoration fund.

Herbert Richardson (the author's great-uncle) working on the carpet shearer at Mackay's, 1929. The shearer removed a fine layer of wool from the pile to give a perfect finish.

Lucy Palmer and Joyce Lightfoot inspecting finished carpets at the factory, *c.* 1950. As far back as the 1920s Mackay's had offices in London, Manchester, Birmingham, Belfast, Glasgow, Melbourne and Sydney.

The factory was partly destroyed in an arson attack by an employee, May 1969. To the left of the picture is Martin's Flour Mill and the ice-rink.

Millburngate and the carpet factory site as seen from the tower of St Margaret's Church, Crossgate, 1920s. The old bridge which crossed the mill-race can be seen to the left of the picture, right of the large chimney. Blagdon's Leather Works are on the left; in the centre is Martin's Flour Mill; and on the right part of Mackay's carpet factory can be seen.

15
Licensed Premises

Mr James Elliot, landlord of the Sun Inn,
34 Hallgarth Street, c. 1933. Mr Elliott was
also a prison warder at Durham. The Sun Inn
is now a private house.

Old Elvet, looking towards Elvet Bridge, showing the Waterloo and the County Hotels on the right, 1860s. The County Hotel brickwork is shown before it was plastered over. To the left of the photograph is the old Durham City Working Men's Club, which was previously the Wheatsheaf Inn (see opposite page). Later, in 1897, it became the Royal Mail Inn, and in 1898 the Cycle Hotel.

A close-up view of the Working Men's Club, 2 Old Elvet, *c.* 1904. The property was pulled down in about 1904 and four small retail shops were built on the site (see page 140).

The Pineapple Inn, Old Durham Gardens, *c.* 1910. The landlord at the time was Mr J. Clifford. A public right of way still exists through Old Durham Gardens.

The Tanners' Arms, 48 Framwellgate, 1950s. The public house was situated on the left-hand side going up Framwellgate Peth.

The Blue Bell Inn, 98 Framwellgate, *c.* 1960. It was one of the last properties to be demolished for the new road system in the early 1960s.

The Wearmouth Bridge Hotel, 17 Claypath, 1960s. The old gas showrooms can be seen to the right.

The staff of the Wearmouth Bridge Hotel, 17 Claypath, 1920s.

The Wheatsheaf staff and customers, 17 July 1954. Back row, left to right: Mr and Mrs Burnip, -?-. Front row: Benny Bradley, Minnie Snowdon.

A Leek Club party at the Wheatsheaf, 3 Claypath, *c.* 1958.

The Rose & Crown Hotel, Market Place (now Woolworths) decorated for the Diamond Jubilee of Queen Victoria, 1897. The manager William MacFarlane and his staff can be seen on the left. The Rose & Crown had a history going back to 1633, when Charles I was presented with silver plate there by the Freemen of the City.

The Royal Hotel, Co-operative Terrace, 1960s. This area was demolished to make way for the through road from Millburngate to the top of North Road.

The Railway Hotel, which stood to the right of the Royal Hotel, 1960s. This was demolished at the same time as the Royal Hotel, for the new through road.

The King's Arms Hotel, 105 Claypath, 1960s. This building stood to the left of what is now Boots the Chemist, along with many other shops. These were demolished in the early 1960s for the new through road.

The Station Hotel, which stood at the top of North Road, 1960s. It also had to make way for the through road.

The Market Hotel, Market Place, 1919. The small white sign in the window reads 'No Ladies Supplied'. It was here on 20 November 1869 that the Durham Miners' Association was formed.

Mr Robert Robertson, landlord, standing outside the old Woodman Inn, 23 Gilesgate, *c.* 1920. It was pulled down and rebuilt in the 1920s. This building dated from the early eighteenth century. A stone lintel from the old inn was placed above the new back door; it reads 'G.M. 1715'.

The Maltman Hotel, 29 Claypath, 1960s. The building is now a cycle shop. To the left is the old Palladium cinema, which was built and owned by the Holliday family. The cinema has stood empty for many years; it was last used as a bingo hall.

New Durham Working Men's Club's first Leek Show, September 1958. Left to right: Mr R. Gleason, Harry Wills, -?-, Bob Fairless, -?-, Jack Mollon, Bill Hann, Tommy Thompson. Jack Mollon was the first gardener to win the New Durham and District Club Leek Trophy.

The old Three Horse Shoes, 16 Sunderland Road, *c.* 1920. To the right of the building is the old Coach Opening, which got its name from the Railway Coach – a name previously given to the Three Horse Shoes.

The Bay Horse Inn, 110 Gilesgate, in the 1930s. It has now been rebuilt and renamed the Durham Light Infantryman. Behind the Bay Horse stood Lockerbie's shoeing forge (see page 150).

The old Hare & Hounds, 39 Sunderland Road, early 1960s. To the left can be seen the building of the present-day Hare & Hounds. Left to right: Tommy Dance, Joe Barker and the landlord, Matty Cooper.

The Bay Horse Inn, West Sherburn, *c.* 1910. The landlord, Edwin Bamlett, is standing in the doorway. The inn is now known as The Tavern. The old road to Sherburn once passed the inn before the new motorway bridge was built in the 1960s.

The Grange Inn, Carrville, named after the nearby Grange Iron Works, *c.* 1924. The photograph shows Evelyn, Jack and William, the children of the landlord, William Graymorrow.

16
Defence of the Realm

Bugler Walter Shea, proudly wearing his dress uniform of the 8th Durham Light Infantry (Territorials), c. 1922. Walter spent all his working life at Mackay's Carpet Factory.
He wrote Carpet-Making *in Durham City.*

Sergeants of the 2nd North Durham Militia, standing outside the main door of the Militia Barracks (now Vane Tempest Hall), *c.* 1874. The barracks were built in 1864; the militia had previously had their headquarters in Church Street, opposite St Oswald's Church.

Sergeant Thomas Beeby, *c.* 1901. Born in Gilesgate, he was a groom when he joined the 4th Durham Light Infantry (Militia) in 1887, aged nineteen. He soon rose to the rank of sergeant and served in the Boer War, attached to the 3rd Durham Light Infantry (Militia). In 1901 he was awarded the DCM, the only soldier from the 4th Durham Light Infantry to receive this medal. He died in Sherburn House Hospital in July 1910, from tuberculosis.

An official 'Welcome Home' reception, marching down North Road in the direction of Framwellgate Bridge, *c.* 1919. The King William public house stands on the right. The officer leading centre (of the front row) is Colonel Turnbull of the 8th Battalion Durham Light Infantry.

The 5th Durham Voluntary Aid Hospital (VAH), in the North Bailey (now Cranmer Hall), *c.* 1915. Many of the first Voluntary Aid Detachment (VAD) members were former suffragettes. The gentleman with his arm bandaged is Joseph Pattison of Ivy Cottage, near Brown's Boat House.

'B' Company, Durham Royal Garrison Artillery, during the First World War. They are seen here at the Barracks, Gilesgate (Vane Tempest Hall). In December 1931 the barracks were put up for sale by auction by Mr J.W. Wood, on behalf of the owner, the Marquess of Londonderry.

The First World War tank in Wharton Park, *c.* 1926. The tank was presented by the National War Savings Association in appreciation of local efforts. On 10 June 1919 it arrived at Gilesgate Goods station. Tank No. 2783 was one of the original tanks to be used in the First World War; it first saw action at Vimy Ridge and later at Arras. It was officially handed over to the city at Wharton Park on 17 June 1919.

'B' Squadron, Northumberland Hussars, Rifle Team, *c.* 1927. 'B' Squadron were based at the Barracks (Vane Tempest Hall). Most of the men were local, and in the 1920s they had a waiting list of 100 young men waiting to join. The photograph shows the winners of the Territorial Army Rifle Associations Competitions 1926–27. Top row, left to right: Tprs. T.D. Thompson, A. Saborn, L/Cpl. J. Brice, Tpr J.P. Nichol. Middle row: Tprs. G.W. Lightburn, W. Allison, R.O. Sutton, T. Stoddart, M. Blackburn, J. Harris, E. Geary, W. Dunmore, A. Sharp. Front row: Farrier E. Shepherd, L/Sgt. C. Roberts, F/Sgt. W. Telford, S.S.M. H. Lee, Capt. C. Vaux. M.C. (Squadron Leader), Sgt. W.H. Crees (PSI), Sgts. T. Halliday, M. Thompson, L/Cpl. A. Baldwin.

PC Dick Collinson on duty in the first police-box, 1940. It is interesting to see the wartime issue tin helmet. This police-box appeared in the early 1930s, and became a landmark in the city. It was demolished in 1957 and was replaced by the second police-box (see page 186).

ARP (Air Raid Precautions) Wardens on duty at Gilesgate, *c*. 1942. The photograph was taken in the grounds of the old 'Gate' School, which became St Giles' church hall (St Giles' filling station is built on the site). The warden in the middle is Mr Tom Robinson, of 1 Malvern Terrace, Gilesgate.

Durham City Auxiliary Fire Service, *c*. 1940. The photograph was taken on the Sands, at the bottom of Providence Row. Top row, left to right: Firemen ? Bunker, J. Green, B. Hammill, M. Carrol. Front row: B. Blakey, J. Armstrong, T. Clish, W. Wills, Colonel Officer J. Willis, G. Shannon, Leading Fireman C. Brown and Section Leader N. Murray.

Durham City Observer Corps, 14 December 1944. The headquarters stood behind the old post office in Providence Row. Top row, left to right: Betty Newby, Enid Garnham. Middle row: Margery Gavin, Mary Morrison. Front row: Nora Weavers, Dorothy Meade, Betty MacIntyre, Rhona Robson, Irene Richardson, Daisy Armstrong and Mona Taylor.

The 8th Durham Light Infantry, Pioneer Corp, British Expeditionary Force, 1940. The soldier behind the axes in the centre is Tommy Bond (Pioneer Sergeant).

Durham City Home Guard on the steps of Durham Castle, *c.* 1945.

A royal visit to Durham Castle during the Second World War, *c.* 1943. King George and Queen Elizabeth are seen leaving.

Neville's Cross students, who were transferred to Bede College at the beginning of the Second World War, seen entering the air raid shelter, *c.* 1940. Neville's Cross College was taken over by the War Office as a casualty clearing station.

Regimental Bicentenary Parade, 17 May 1958. The Flag's colour party is seen marching towards the entrance of the old Drill Hall (home of the 8th Battalion Durham Light Infantry) at the bottom of Gilesgate Bank. The Drill Hall was officially opened on 7 February 1902. It was built by Messrs Jasper Kell & Sons, North Road, Durham City; the architect was J. Oswald & Son, of Newcastle.

Territorials from the 8th Battalion Durham Light Infantry walking back from the Cathedral after an Armistice Parade at the Cathedral, 1974. Leading the parade is Major J. Jackson, followed by Captain Robinson and Company-Sergeant Major C. Armstrong.

VE day party at the Duck Pond, Gilesgate, May 1945. The building in the background is Gilesgate Methodist Church. The young child sitting on a woman's knee in the front row on the left is Doretta Savage, the author's mother.

17
Durham at Prayer

*Bishop Hensley Henson, photographed by John
Edis, c. 1929. Dean of Durham 1913–18;
Bishop of Hereford 1918–20; Bishop of
Durham 1920–39. His consecration had been
strongly opposed by Anglo-Catholics. As Bishop
of Durham he became increasingly liberal in his
churchmanship, and took a notable part in
national ecclesiastical conflicts.*

The burnt-out ruins of Sherburn Hospital Chapel after the fire, December 1864. The Revd J. Carr, Master of the Hospital, had banked up the fire on the evening of Saturday 3 December to warm the church for Sunday, but the flue had become blocked; wood panelling caught fire in the early hours of Sunday morning.

The Congregational Chapel, Claypath, *c.* 1880. This building still survives, tucked away behind the United Reformed Church.

A typical Durham house, 1885. This house, 48 Claypath, was (for a short time) the residence of Alfred Tucker when he was curate of St Nicholas' Church. He later went on to become the first Bishop of Uganda, 1899–1911.

An unusual view of St Margaret's Church, Crossgate, in the 1890s. The church dates from around 1160. The font is twelfth-century and is of Frosterley Marble. Originally part of St Oswald's parish, this church served the residents of the Borough of Crossgate. Burials were not permitted here until 1431. Sir John Duck, the Durham Dick Whittington, is buried here along with members of the Shafto family.

The remains of the old Wesleyan Chapel, Rotten Row (Court Lane), 1920s. It was here that John Wesley preached on a number of occasions when he visited Durham. The chapel was established in 1770. The building was demolished in the 1940s. In 1808 a new chapel was built in Chapel Passage, Old Elvet, and in 1904 the Elvet Methodist Church was built.

St Hild's Chapel, *c.* 1913. It is rarely seen, as it is tucked away in the grounds of St Hild's College surrounded by student accommodation. It was built by John Shepherd of Gilesgate, and was dedicated on 14 June 1913.

Harvest Festival, Houghall Mission, 1920s. This corrugated iron building was in the parish of St Oswald's. It served the small community of Houghall, which at one time was a thriving mining village.

The congregation of the Jubilee Primitive Methodist Chapel at the centenary celebrations of the founding of the society (1824–1924) at Wharton Park.

The Jubilee Primitive Methodist Chapel, North Road, *c.* 1961. The Iceland freezer shop now occupies this site. On 19 May 1861 the Jubilee Church was opened. Before that date the congregation had been meeting in a small chapel in Back Silver Street.

An early engraving of St Giles' Church, 1824. It was drawn by Joseph Bouet (1791–1856), the French artist who taught art and French at Durham School.

Acknowledgements

So many people have donated photographs to the Gilesgate Archive that it is impossible to thank them individually. Institutions which have helped include:

Durham University Library, Palace Green; Durham City Reference Library; Durham Arts, Libraries & Museums Department; Durham County Council; the trustees of the Durham Light Infantry Museum & Mr I. Forsyth.

Without this assistance this book would never have been possible and the author acknowledges it gratefully. If any reader has new material or information, it would be helpful if contact could be made with:

Michael Richardson, 128 Gilesgate, Durham DH1 1QG (0191–384–1427).

Index